# Trade the Trader

## Know Your Competition and Find Your Edge for Profitable Trading

Quint Tatro

Vice President, Publisher: Tim Moore
Associate Publisher and Director of Marketing: Amy Neidlinger
Executive Editor: Jim Boyd
Editorial Assistant: Pamela Boland
Development Editor: Russ Hall
Operations Manager: Gina Kanouse
Senior Marketing Manager: Julie Phifer
Publicity Manager: Laura Czaja
Assistant Marketing Manager: Megan Colvin
Cover Designer: Alan Clements
Managing Editor: Kristy Hart
Project Editor: Betsy Harris
Copy Editor: Keith Cline
Proofreader: Kathy Ruiz
Indexer: Erika Millen
Senior Compositor: Gloria Schurick
Manufacturing Buyer: Dan Uhrig

© 2011 by Pearson Education, Inc.
Publishing as FT Press
Upper Saddle River, New Jersey 07458

**This book is sold with the understanding that neither the author nor the publisher is engaged in rendering legal, accounting, or other professional services or advice by publishing this book. Each individual situation is unique. Thus, if legal or financial advice or other expert assistance is required in a specific situation, the services of a competent professional should be sought to ensure that the situation has been evaluated carefully and appropriately. The author and the publisher disclaim any liability, loss, or risk resulting directly or indirectly, from the use or application of any of the contents of this book.**

Charts courtesy of Worden—www.Worden.com.

FT Press offers excellent discounts on this book when ordered in quantity for bulk purchases or special sales. For more information, please contact U.S. Corporate and Government Sales, 1-800-382-3419, corpsales@pearsontechgroup.com. For sales outside the U.S., please contact International Sales at international@pearson.com.

Company and product names mentioned herein are the trademarks or registered trademarks of their respective owners.

Printed in the United States of America

First Printing October 2010

ISBN-10: 0-13-706708-9
ISBN-13: 978-0-13-706708-4

Pearson Education LTD.
Pearson Education Australia PTY, Limited.
Pearson Education Singapore, Pte. Ltd.
Pearson Education Asia, Ltd.
Pearson Education Canada, Ltd.
Pearson Educación de Mexico, S.A. de C.V.
Pearson Education—Japan
Pearson Education Malaysia, Pte. Ltd.

Library of Congress Cataloging-in-Publication Data

Tatro, Quint, 1977-

Trade the trader : know your competition and find your edge for profitable trading / Quint Tatro.

p. cm.

ISBN-13: 978-0-13-706708-4 (hardcover : alk. paper)

ISBN-10: 0-13-706708-9

1. Investment analysis. 2. Technical analysis (Investment analysis) 3. Portfolio management. I. Title.

HG4529.T38 2011

332.64—dc22

2010027306

*To traders: May you always embrace the tape.*

# Contents

# Acknowledgments

I first want to give the glory to my Lord within whom I can do all things.

To my wife who is always my rock whether it be to keep me grounded or keep me standing tall. I love you more than ever and appreciate more than you know the patience you have had while I have been on this journey.

To my children who were also patient with me while I spent many weekends writing. May you always give 110% to all the tasks before you and never stop dreaming.

To my mother who believed in my writing long before a book was ever in the making. Your humility, dedication, and perseverance have made me the man I am today. For that I am forever grateful.

To my father who opened my eyes to the world of finance, big dreams, and fortitude. It has been an honor to be a recipient of your wisdom.

To 'Rev,' who took me under his wing and graciously opened my eyes to the world of pattern recognition and double-meat sandwiches.

I would like to thank some dear friends who also continue to believe in me regardless of my multiple shortcomings:

Steve McBroom—You have been a father figure to me for years, and I continue to learn from you daily. Thank you for always believing in me and making sure I know it.

Anne Beaucage—I cannot imagine where I would be without your guidance. You led by example, and I will forever attempt to mimic your actions.

Prakash—You have become one of my best friends. I am continuously in awe of all that you believe I am capable of. Your continuous challenge makes me a better trader, a better man, and a better friend. For that I am grateful.

To the people at FT Press: Your professional guidance with this project was fantastic. It was an honor and a pleasure to work with you all.

# About the Author

**Quint Tatro** is President and owner of Tatro Capital, LLC, a premier fee-based investment advisory firm located in Central Kentucky. Although the firm may be located hundreds of miles from Wall Street, Quint is regarded as one of the 'Street's' best technicians and has frequented such shows as CNBC's *Fast Money* and Fox Business's *Happy Hour*, to relay his thoughts and ideas. In addition, Quint writes columns for financial websites such as Forbes.com, Minyanville.com, StockTwits.com, FinancialSense.com, and Tickerville.com

Financial management runs in the genes for Quint, as he comes from a family that has been involved in the financial world for more than 100 years. Long before he could ever officially be employed, he assisted his father, a 38-year veteran money manager, with various projects including research and economic forecasting. Gaining his official start in the business in 1999, Quint began as a retail broker in the family firm located in Rochester, New York. Rapidly growing his business, in 2000 he relocated to Lexington, Kentucky, and in 2003 he separated from the family firm, spreading his wings and launching Tatro Capital.

Furthering his experience and education, in 2005 Quint was given the incredible opportunity to serve as a general partner in a hedge fund located in Bradenton, Florida. During this time period, Quint assisted in the management of a $60 million fund and daily operations of the entire business. In 2007, Quint once again found himself heading back to the Blue Grass to reestablish Tatro Capital and make his now distinguished services available to the general public.

Quint hails from upstate New York but left in 1996 to attend the University of Kentucky where he graduated cum laude with a degree in finance. In 2004 he married his college sweetheart Brandie, who has left the field of physical therapy to enroll as a full-time mom raising their children.

Quint and Brandie are active members of Southland Christian Church and each posses a unique heart for missions, particularly the region of northwest Haiti.

# chapter 1

# I'm Trading Against You

I sat in front of my six screens like a hawk high on a limb, watching the flickering symbols race across my level-two quote box. Market breadth had been horrible all day, notching 5 – 1 decliners over advancers, capping off a week that looked as if the indices would finish close to 5% in the red. I had been nailing the short side all week and was ready to book hefty gains against unsuspecting latecomers and amateur traders who actually believe they have a leg up with their basic technical analysis. I sifted through countless charts, and each one walked a very fine line, looking as if at any moment they would plunge to their deaths, cratering into the abyss. I imagined the number of traders cuing up these exact charts for shorts, and I shook my head again at what would surely be their misfortune. For a moment, I remembered what it felt like to be in their shoes. I recalled the days when I felt empowered by my basic chart knowledge. It would be a time such as this that I would believe the moons had aligned for a perfect trade, a trade that would correspond with all that I had learned from basic trading, netting me huge profits. Unfortunately, over the years it became clear that basic strategy no longer was enough. I had witnessed time and again how the basics would work for only a moment, at which point an immediate change of character would set in, robbing me of my hard-earned capital. This time was different. This time I sat with the hawks, not with the unsuspecting squirrels gathering their charts like nuts, moments before those nuts were snatched up and taken away by a bigger, craftier prey. The same stage had been set this time, the players identical, and even though I already knew an incredible bounce was forthcoming, the exciting anticipation continued to build.

The market had been moving methodically lower all day. However, subtle signs told me to prepare for yet another play on those who equip themselves with sticks in a fight only won by bazookas and heavy tanks. I sat observing how the S&P 500 was bouncing back and forth, grasping for a bottom, when in reality it looked as if another breakdown was a foregone conclusion. Each rally attempt was met with selling, and each move back into the extremely short-term base seemed to be with more vigor and intensity than the one before.

I again pondered what most traders would be thinking as they observed the action and lined up the stocks they would short on yet another thrust lower. I could almost feel their passion through the tape as I watched the intensity build. I noted in my chat room how I had not yet seen the "towel trade" and until I did, I would believe new lows were pending, with a better opportunity to cover and book profits. Many in the room I had traded with for years and knew that the "towel trade" was merely my way of describing the move at which point most traders throw in the towel and, in this case, either give up on their longs or press their shorts. The congruent force sparking a breathtaking move, yet one that would only last a moment. Most in my chat room had been on a similar journey as I, and had finally arrived at the place where we were in a position to profit from the towel trade, instead of being the ones throwing in the towels.

The clock struck noon, and while a rumble in my stomach reminded me that I hadn't eaten anything since beginning my day around 4:45 a.m., I couldn't yet leave the screens until the trade had been executed with the money in the bank. I sifted through all my various charts, again noting that not one looked bullish, nor did any indicator I followed (such as breadth or sector leadership), yet I refused to be the greater fool. I had no intentions of playing the hero, throwing hard-earned capital at a declining market hoping for a bounce, but I knew very well that just when everyone moved to one side believing that a continued move into the abyss was a foregone conclusion, a change was imminent. This was the trade I was waiting for.

Even though I had seen the trade play out hundreds of times before, it never got dull. Finally, after observing the market for almost four hours, the drop began. At first it started in a slow and methodical fashion as the recent support gave way and traders realized what was happening. Within seconds, my alert box started to trigger stock after stock that was breaking below a predetermined level, of which I acted on not a single one. Rather than add new shorts, I watched closely as my existing inventory started to show even a greater profit, and one by one, stocks began a rapid and vicious decline. I was curious what was happening among the masses, so I took a quick glance at the StockTwits Twitter screen. As I suspected, trader after trader was adding short inventory almost as fast as their arrogance grew over what they believed to be certain riches. I covered half of my shorts and watched as the speed of the decline increased with the S&P losing a quick 5 points. I wondered whether a lull would set in, as traders

3

regrouped, but in a blink of an eye another 5 points had disappeared, and that was my cue to exit my shorts completely and go straight to cash. One by one, my stocks vanished off my screen while the realized profit column grew with my extracted funds. It was only 2:30 or so in the afternoon, but I was done for the day, with one month's worth of profits in the bank, and it was only the 5th of February.

The move was what I had been waiting for all week, and was my cue to take profits and start the weekend early. My timing wasn't exact, but within the hour on that Friday, the market started to reverse in a rapid fashion, repairing all of the almost 2% decline it had seen during the day, to close positive, squeezing the accounts of the unsuspecting traders yet again.

You would have to be living under a rock not to see the trading wave sweeping the nation as average investors move in mass toward the world of stock speculation. Not only are they fed up with the traditional Wall Street advisory practice, but they've been burned studying balance sheets and listening to management and are not interested in buying the next great American franchise at a deep discount, for a longer-term hold. No, these educated individuals are searching out and learning the core principals of technical analysis, behavioral economics, and even the likes of momentum investing. As they learn, they quickly see the real potential for riches. However, just as quickly as the number of people moving toward this field grows, the landscape shifts, with the greatest profit potential coming not from just trading the market, but from *trading the traders*.

You see, what most investors don't understand as they start to learn their basic technical patterns, such as cup and handle breakouts, or as they study their MACD (Moving Average Convergence / Divergence) or RSI (Relative Strength Index) indicators, is they are the ones actually in play. Seasoned traders are no longer just cuing off of charts or indicators, they are also analyzing those same charts to determine what the amateurs are doing, and are seeking to profit from the ignorance of the newcomers. It's a chess game where the successful traders are thinking two and three moves ahead, playing off the basic strategy of the newcomers. Those simply pursuing a basic path of understanding technical analysis will find it is a road that ultimately leads to frustration, whereas those looking to trade the traders will be met with an endless world of opportunity.

It took me a long time to figure this out, and before I did, I was the trader licking my chops at the number of shorts setting up on a Friday afternoon whoosh, as I just described, only to lose my shirt on the reversal. You see, in that specific example, three levels of traders are present, with most occupying the first two areas:

- **Level one:**   Although level one has dramatically thinned out after the 2008 bear market, there are still those who believe jumping in to catch a falling safe is the prudent way to go. In my example, this group would have been buying the market the entire way down, losing their shirts along the way, and were the ones throwing in stocks at any price during the towel trade mentioned earlier.

- **Level two:**   The second level is the unsuspecting, semi-educated trader who realizes buying sunken ships is a loser's game and knows that shorting them is the way to profits. This trader stalks his prey, and relies on basic technical analysis or other advanced indicators to tell him when it's time to move in. For our previous example, this is the trader who shorted on the towel trade believing the breaks would continue to plummet.

- **Level three:** Level three is not occupied by many investors. However, this is the group who more than likely has already moved through level one and level two, understanding that it isn't just economic forces or corporate profits that move stocks but that it is the traders acting in concert who create market movement. They thus understand what traders are thinking and doing, which gives them a greater edge toward capturing profits.

Traders are always in a state of flux when it comes to the way they approach the market. I believe this is so because it is real money and potential profits or losses that are involved, and therefore everyone is always attempting to glean a new edge. The market is quick to grade your approach in that it only takes seconds before you know whether or not your strategy was correct. Because of this rapid evaluation, traders are more inclined to move quickly to change, seeking out a better and more appropriate way to approach their investing. From my vantage point, the masses are moving to a strategy that involves some sort of technical analysis or indicators far away from the basic buy-and-hold approach of traditional Wall Street. As a result of the vast number of people shifting to this strategy, it is becoming saturated to the point that it rarely works as effectively as it once did. To truly succeed in trading, you need to seek out another level, not only possessing a basic foundation and proven edge, but also seeking to understand the movement of others and how to profit from this. If you do not grasp the theme of trading the trader, you will have a frustrating career in stock speculation, regardless of how passively or methodically you approach the business. It's really quite simple: If you are following technical analysis, you are either stalking the movement of others, or your movements are being stalked. If you don't know on which side you fall, odds are you are someone's next meal.

# chapter 2

# My Story

My journey into what I consider successful trading was quite similar to what most traders experience, except for the fact that I was exposed to the financial world at quite an early age. One can debate whether this early exposure was, in fact, beneficial. Over the years, I have come to realize that it is easier to learn a successful trading style if you approach the subject with little to no understanding of other strategies. It is always my preference to guide someone through the world of successful trading who does not possess any financial background and therefore no preconceived notions or investment bias. Nonetheless, I am very proud to have been raised by a successful investment manager, which resulted in financial discussions being commonplace around the dinner table. Whereas my early education resulted from osmosis, it wasn't until years later that a brief chat with my father set me on a path that now finds me sharing what I have learned with you.

I was in high school at the time, and I can still vividly recall the conversation. My father and I sat in the living room, having just finished watching a classic movie (an evening ritual). I turned to him and asked, "Dad, how can I make 10 million dollars?" Mind you, while both my father and mother imparted many pearls of wisdom along the way, it was his response that evening that I value more than he'll ever know. Most parents, when asked something like this by their children, might chuckle and perhaps make an offhanded comment about winning the lottery or maybe a suggestion to "marry well." Paradoxically, even though we have little difficulty telling our children that they can be anything that they want to be in life, I doubt that few would take a question like this seriously. However, one look at my face and my father could tell that I was not joking. At that age, my ideas were simple, and despite having an excellent jump shot and a mean crossover, I knew that my chances in the NBA were about one in a gazillion. I didn't want to waste my time and energy doing something that wasn't going to reap some serious fruit. My father didn't bat an eye, and with a sense of pride he said to me, "You can make 10 million dollars in the stock market." Well, that was that, and from that point forward I set my sights on achieving a goal to become financially successful through the trading of stocks.

Now, it certainly would be colorful if I could relate that I then attended an Ivy League college followed by a brief but extremely successful stint as an investment banker, which led to becoming a billion-dollar hedge fund manager. After all, isn't that the path taken by all successful traders? Not quite. After high school, I said goodbye to upstate New York and embarked on a state education at the University of Kentucky, where I was inducted into the world of what I like to call academic finance. While I learned the basic vocabulary of the financial world, my real education in the financial markets would come years later. My final year in college was a rocky one because I had thrown myself completely into an Internet start-up that failed miserably when the technology boom went bust. While the experience of my first real business venture was a tough pill to swallow, it instilled in me a sense of humility that I carry to this day. It was through this failure I learned just how elusive success can be, and I began to grasp the value and importance of managing risk. In 2000, I left Kentucky and headed home to Rochester, New York, to nurture the seed that was planted during that earlier conversation with my father. It was then that I became a stockbroker.

My first experience in the brokerage business was typical. I was given a phone, a list of names, and a pitch. The difference was that I wasn't selling a stock idea. Instead, I was pitching a seminar wherein the prospective investors would learn all about what our firm had to offer to meet their estate-planning needs. It didn't take long before the wind came out of my sails and my energy level waned. Even though I was like a starry-eyed kid around the flicker of the ticker, I just couldn't get excited about financial or estate planning. In less than a year, I decided that a move back to Kentucky was in the cards. With a little money in my pocket and a new bounce in my step, I figured that opening my own brokerage office in Kentucky was the next logical move. Again, my ideas were simple. I believed if I was the proprietor of my own business I could choose the direction as I saw fit, thus moving closer toward my goal of true money management.

The year was 2001, and my plug for new clients was, "Sell everything." Most investors were still disillusioned by what was happening in the markets, although they believed that the then bear market was nothing more than a mere correction. This was an opportunity to scoop up depressed tech stocks, they thought, shares of companies they knew little about. It was at this point that my passion for equities and investing started to shine. Like many who have entered this field, I sought to utilize the same educational tools of others. From early on, I was taught that Warren Buffett was the pillar of investment success and that his strategy was by far the best method available for securing wealth in the market. Believing this, I devoured everything on the subject that I could, even going so far as to read and reread *The Intelligent Investor,* the fundamental investment bible written by Benjamin Graham and David Dodd. Learning how to calculate intrinsic value and the importance of remaining extremely patient while waiting for opportunities to present themselves wasn't all that hard. Furthermore, it wasn't that difficult to understand that valuations during the tech frenzy were out of control and that, in fact, a reversion to the mean would be coming soon. I made a calculated decision that the best opportunity I had for building a business at this time was by bucking the trend of other advisors who were attempting to calm their clients by suggesting that they ride out the storm. Being very young and having a relatively small list of clients for references didn't make it easy for me to obtain new business. This was especially so when you consider that my strategy was a bit brash, since we would begin the client relationship by going completely to cash and then remain that way for the next several months. Luckily, a few took a shot with me, which laid the foundation for a successful business as the markets continued to plummet and we stayed sidelined. It was then that I learned just how valuable capital preservation can be.

As time passed and the tech bubble burst, stocks retreated from beyond the stratosphere, and eventually incredible values became apparent. I would like to say that it was at this point I went all in on deeply discounted value stocks and thus secured the first fortune of my career, but that would be untrue. Although I did allocate funds back into the market, I did so at a very tepid rate.

And even though I had a few good years as the market recovered, I realized quickly that I still had no real clue what I was doing. Sure, I had proven I knew how to buy low and sell high, but managing funds through the ups and downs of an increasingly volatile marketplace was still foreign to me. I decided that it was time to pursue a serious education in trading.

If nothing else, the sheer volume of Jim Cramer's voice was tough to ignore. His popularity was growing, and it wasn't long before anywhere you looked, there he was talking about the markets in a way few outside of Wall Street had ever witnessed. At the time, his radio broadcast was syndicated in Kentucky, and once I got a taste of this style that seemed so fresh, I didn't miss a show. It makes no difference how I view his material now; the simple fact is that Jim Cramer was instrumental in bringing trading to the masses, and he was a major force in influencing my career as a trader. The minute that I became exposed to what Jim was teaching, I was sold. I remember heading to the bookstore as soon as I could, buying a copy of his book and devouring it the next day. It was as if the world I had always been craving was revealed to me and Jim Cramer had opened the door. Naturally, I gravitated to his daily writings on his website, TheStreet.com, and it wasn't long before I paid for a subscription to his journal on Real Money and eventually became an Action Alerts Plus subscriber. I soaked up everything I could, reading his daily posts three and four times, studying the companies he was tracking, and investing personal funds in the stocks listed in his subscription portfolio. At the time, one thing I enjoyed about Jim was that he always seemed to be where I was, emotionally. This, of course, was solely dependent on how the market performed that day. If the market was up, I was happy, and so was Jim. I could expect a virtual high five after the close and an extremely positive radio show. However, if the market was down, it was a safe bet that I was depressed, and I could tell that he was also frustrated. Despite the ups and downs, he did a fantastic job of motivating his followers to stay in the game and encouraged us all to pull ourselves back up again for the next day. I accepted this emotional roller coaster as part of the game, taking it at face value that the moods of all successful market participants correlated with the ups and downs of the market itself. Over time, I quickly learned that this roller coaster was exhausting and, for me at least, unsustainable.

Although Jim stoked the passion that had been inside me for many years, the emotion itself was not translating into market success, and soon I was searching for a new teacher. During my foray into Jim's world of online blogging, I was exposed to another trader and author whose material was exceptional, refreshing, and above all, unemotional. Rev Shark, as he was known on the Web, seemed to take a humble approach to the market, and I was quickly drawn to his style of allowing the market to tell him what to do (instead of imposing his beliefs on the market). Rather than riding the emotional roller coaster and anticipating its next move, Rev seemed to always be taking a much more reactionary approach, one that was appealing to me. He never seemed to have trouble sitting on the sidelines if he didn't have a good feel. When favorable conditions emerged, however, he would attack quickly. After reading his columns for several months and applying much of his method with great success, I felt compelled to reach out to Rev and let him know just how much I appreciated his work.

Rev Shark and I began exchanging email in which we discussed the markets, individual stocks, and trading strategies. He introduced me to the likes of Bill O'Neil and *Investor's Business Daily* and to the works of Nicholas Darvas and Richard Smitten. He expressed a desire to help me learn, and when I realized he was open to dialogue, I wasted no time absorbing as much as I could. Over the next several months, our relationship evolved to the point where I started to contemplate whether a business opportunity were possible. After much prayer and contemplation, I ultimately submitted to him a business proposal for a joint venture. Lo and behold, in the summer of 2005, I was off on a new adventure as my wife and I relocated to Florida. I would start working directly with Rev, gaining an education over the next two years that would lay the foundation for everything I did professionally thereafter. From 2005 through 2007, I received what I would call the equivalent of an MBA in trading. If I wasn't buying or selling stocks, I was writing about them. And if I wasn't writing about them, odds are I was thinking about them. My days and nights were literally consumed with all things related to stocks and trading. We had early success, but spent much of 2006 and 2007 fighting an uptrend, during which I learned the importance of grinding it out and about how true market success is a marathon and not a sprint.

As 2007 came to a close, it became apparent that once again it was time for me to move on, taking all that I had learned and applying it firsthand. Although our professional collaboration has since come to an end, Rev Shark will always be one of the greatest professional influences in my life, for the time he spent educating me in all areas of stock speculation. With a solid foundation in place, I left Florida in 2007 and relocated back to Kentucky and reestablished my own firm.

Rev Shark had given me many of the tools that I needed to succeed in the stock market, but I felt that I still had many holes in my game. My approach was artistic in nature, and I wasn't able to articulate well just what my trading style was. I discovered that although I was more successful than many traders, my profits were sporadic at best. I often experienced long winning streaks followed by heavy draws. I had certainly built a firm foundation of knowledge, but I soon realized that I needed to improve both my technique and my execution, and so I set on a course to develop what would eventually become the successful style that I now utilize.

Most traders have the same goal: make money consistently. Many struggle in their pursuit because they bounce from strategy to strategy, failing to first construct a core foundation and then develop a style to adapt to various market conditions. No singular strategy works in every market, yet many traders are searching for that one-size-fits-all method. Given the ever-changing investing landscape and the number of players involved, I believe that is a fruitless, if not a losing, proposition.

Currently, the common belief is that "buy and hold" is no longer viable. I discuss publicly how much I reject this strategy, but who is to say that we won't enter another raging bull market where it works very well? If you abandon the buy-and-hold method, is the alternative plan as simple as trading for the shorter term? If you develop a core foundation based on a buy-and-hold strategy, shouldn't you also be aware in which environment this strategy is inclined to work, instead of believing that it applies to all market conditions? Still, it is not even that simple.

The difference between those who constantly seek a successful strategy and those who experience consistent success is rooted within a system that is timeless and applicable to all markets regardless of market direction. Successful traders, in addition to possessing a strong foundational strategy, are also keenly aware of those with whom they are trading against and among, and they will always be conscious of what the masses are doing, so as to capitalize on the movement of the herd. In short, to be consistently successful in trading, you must be armed with an adaptable style and ever cognizant of the trader landscape.

It has taken me more than ten years to develop the basis of my strategy, and still I continue to hone and adjust, learning every day from the market itself. If you are looking to become successful you will immediately improve your chances if you settle on one system and strive to perfect it instead of changing it depending on your mood, the markets, or your last few trades. It is only after perfecting your system that you will be able to adjust your style to fit a variety of markets and gain an advantage over others.

Although many different stock-speculation strategies exist, I lay out in the following chapters what I believe to be the best one. If you learn and implement this strategy, you will have a much greater chance of attaining whatever stock market goals you have for yourself, be it $1 million or even $10 million. There is no shortcut, and there is no way around the hard work success demands. Those who promise effortless stock market riches do a disservice to the noble and challenging craft of the stock trader. With an open mind, an aptitude to learn, and a heart to practice, you can achieve greatness. However, it will come only with devotion and commitment.

# chapter 3

# It's All Opportunity

Every trader must overcome a certain psychological roadblock before ever making any true progress. That is, every trader who wants to achieve success must accept and embrace this simple yet profound truth: There is no good or bad in the market, simply opportunity. Most people misinterpret the market to be either good or bad as it relates to price action going up or down. If the market advances on a particular day, you assume that the market had a "good day." Conversely, when the market declines, it is said to have had a "bad day." If you subject yourself to the ebbs and flows of the tickertape without taking control of your investments, you will naturally agree with this statement because you will see your investments rise and fall with the market (and thus you will feel good one day, bad the other). The problem with this ingrained assumption is successful and consistent traders must never view the market as good or bad, but rather as a world of opportunity. They must seek to take advantage of the price action regardless of the direction. The moment you stop allowing the general market movement to dictate your emotions, you unleash a powerful world of opportunity that just seeks to capitalize on market movement, rather than be subject to the general direction for a particular day.

I was taught from a young age to seek out solid investment opportunities, buy them, and let them work. So, it took me a long time to truly embrace the philosophy that I could make money even in a stagnant or declining market. It wasn't until I finally removed *good* and *bad* from my vocabulary that I unleashed the power I had to take advantage of any situation available to me on any given day. It sounds simple. Ask yourself if you have, in fact, embraced the world of opportunity that comes with price movement, or whether you are still hoping for a general direction, be up or down, to play out. If deep inside you desire the market to move in a certain direction, you will never truly unlock your ultimate potential, and you will therefore limit your trading performance for as long as you hold this mindset.

Most investors would agree that a market has three states of being: advancing higher, declining lower, or moving sideways. Should you approach the market conditioned only to think that making money is possible when a market advances, you are taking advantage of just one-third, or 33%, of the general market opportunities, and are thus subjecting yourself to an immediate disadvantage. On the other hand, if you are open-minded to profiting from price action alone, regardless of whether it is up or down, you place yourself in a much better position to profit because you open yourself up to the entire market on any given day. The trick, of course, is to remove any and all bias from your inner being. The market does not care what you think, nor does it care where you believe it should go. To truly take advantage of the opportunity that is price action, you must not overlay any bias whatsoever; otherwise, you will immediately be viewing the market one way and allowing the good versus bad mentality to creep back in.

When approaching the market, you must ask yourself a few questions. Do you have a bias toward market direction? That is, before even approaching the buying or selling of stock, do you believe the market will advance or decline? Perhaps you are reading a tremendous amount of negativity in the press and, therefore, believe the stock market should be declining. Or maybe you have just heard about great advancements in the health-care industry and so conclude that those stocks will be benefiting greatly. Or maybe you have just enjoyed a lovely dinner engagement where intelligent people working in the financial industry laid out their case for a particular stock, industry, or a market move in general. This is actually the way most people approach the market, and sadly, it is the way most will lose all their investment dollars. Internal feelings, general consensus, and other people's opinions should never serve as the foundation for your investment strategy. These are all qualitative variables that can be manipulated or skewed to actually fit your own bias. Conversely, a true quantitative system cannot be argued with, and therefore seeks only to capitalize on the opportunities at hand, not on something that *might* transpire.

I often joke to other traders that if I were trading from a remote cabin, far off in the woods with only my charting software, my performance would improve dramatically. Regardless of how hard they try not to, most traders associate some sort of bias with a stock or industry, and thus encounter frustration and derive poor performance. The truth is that those desiring sustained success must consciously lay any bias down if they want to progress. For example, at the time of this writing, most traders believe that commercial real estate companies are suffering greatly and it is only a matter of time before their stocks experience an aggressive sell-off. Much data supports this view, and intelligent people are paraded in front of the camera almost daily to discuss the imminent demise of these companies. However, the stocks themselves do not yet reflect this widely held belief. In fact, early on in the market advance of 2009, these stocks were acting extremely bullish. Even so, most traders discounted their action due to their industry affiliation. Because so many investors viewed this sector as bearish, believing prices would soon be declining, they missed the opportunity that a significant rise in price actually presented. Although in the future these stocks might, in fact, reverse and plummet, there is great money to be made playing the opportunity rather than standing firm in an opinion or investing bias. Throughout my career, I have learned that most investors cannot disassociate themselves from the actual underlying company, nor from their internal bias about where they believe the price should go. Those who can are already in a much different league than those who cannot. Traders who can think like this, simply looking at a pattern as an opportunity regardless of any other investing bias, will immediately and dramatically improve their results.

In early 2005, prior to my time with Rev, I fell prey to this first-hand, learning just how expensive it can be to hold on to a stock because of strong bias. I rode a position in Winn Dixie stock, all the way into its bankruptcy. I recall the experience as if it were yesterday, remembering how I had done due diligence on the fundamental aspects of the company, believing that they were going to reverse course and become a fantastic investment. I had pored over financial documents, listened to conference calls, and visited stores. I believed I had done all the necessary homework and stood firm as the price eroded before my eyes day in and day out. Despite the declining stock value, I remained steadfast and truly believed that I would soon reap a fortune as others eventually realized what a great value the stock was. Finally, after months of an unending decline, my heart sank as I received word that the company would file for bankruptcy protection. All my hard work, and investment dollars, went up in smoke. After this experience, I vowed never again to lean on any investing bias; instead, I would respect only what the market was telling me.

Before you can truly venture into the world of successful stock trading, you must accept this fact: The market is neither good nor bad; it is just a wonderful world of opportunity. Furthermore, it is not your job to determine where it should go. Instead, you want to humbly seek to profit from whatever direction it moves. That is, you want to embrace whatever may come your way and open yourself up completely to the true opportunities presented day in and day out.

# chapter 4

# The Other Traders

After you have firmly grasped that the market is neither good nor bad but simply a world of opportunity, you must begin to embrace the fact that within this world of opportunity are countless traders seeking to capitalize on the same opportunities as you. Some haven't a clue what they are doing, but more and more are learning, studying, and utilizing basic trading strategies, such as traditional technical analysis. To remain one step ahead of this crowd, you must not only study the underlying market character, you also need to study the current market players. The sooner you realize you are trading against other traders and not just the stocks or the market, the better off you will be.

Different market environments call for different strategies. Those investors who remain the most flexible have the opportunity to realize the most profits. Although I am a firm believer that over several years the fundamentals of a company will ultimately determine where its stock price goes, most traders live within much shorter time frames. Your goal is not to just take advantage of the fundamental prospects of a company or market, but the anomalies that present themselves day in and day out, from which great profits may be realized. Typically, these anomalies could be recognized and capitalized on through traditional technical analysis. Now, however, you must be familiar enough with traditional methods so that you have the confidence to trade among the traders who sometimes overwhelm a method to the point of failure.

You should look no further than 2009 as a reminder of just how important it is to focus on the actions of others when approaching your trades. Coming off one of the worst annual declines the market had seen in decades, 2009 started off no differently as the market quickly dropped more than 25% within the first two months. Broad complacency over stock prices led to a national panic, at which time investors everywhere sold stocks at any price to secure the little money that was left within their accounts. Looking back, I am not sure whether I will ever see anything like the first two and a half months of 2009. However, the experience throughout the remainder of the year left a lasting impression on me.

After a steep decline to start 2009, it was widely accepted that at some point an oversold bounce would set in. When the March 6th bottom arrived and the bounce began, it was a broad belief that the move up would be nothing more than a dead cat, oversold bounce, that would ultimately either lead to new lows or a significant double bottom, which traders could accept as the final gasp of the bear market. Unfortunately, neither scenario played out, and for the remaining nine months, traders were forced to accept a different paradigm that I believe set the stage for a new style of trading never before seen in our history. Despite net mutual fund withdrawals and an overwhelming shift from stocks to bonds, the S&P 500 finished the year up a staggering 23%. This number is even more impressive considering that at one point in the year the market was down more than 25%. You might assume that this meteoric rise gave way to vast fortunes within the trading world, when in reality this is far from the truth. Of the traders who used traditional technical analysis to move them out of the market before the 2008 decline, very few capitalized in the manner the market moved in 2009. Investors who did capitalize on the returns of 2009 were more often than not passive. They were investors who had also suffered incredible losses in 2008 and were simply returning to a level their accounts had been at halfway through the decline itself. When 2009 came to an end, most traders expressed that they were too cautious and not willing to embrace higher prices. I doubt many went any further to study the character of the market at that time, which led to this general theme of extreme caution. I would argue that despite any hind-sight resolutions, if 2009 were to repeat itself in the same manner, most traders would adhere to the same caution, struggling to embrace the move just as before. I believe this is because few investors will ever understand the true nature in which the move itself transpired.

One of the basic tenets of technical analysis is its attempt to study the footprint of institutions so that you may actually see what the larger mutual funds' money is doing as they move in and out of stocks. Traditionally, through this study, you could learn enough about money flow to hop along for the ride. Looking back over 2009, you must ask the question how such a steep rise was possible, when there were actually net mutual fund redemptions. Meaning how is it possible for a market to advance more than 20% when more money moved out of the market than in?

While the return was impressive within itself, the character of the ascent along with the characteristics of the traders must be studied because the move transpired in a technical manner that had never been seen before.

Most traders would agree that throughout 2009, there weren't many significant pullbacks, yet those that arrived developed in such a way as to infer lower prices were on the horizon and, as a result, these were incredibly challenging to accept as prudent points of entry for going long. A basic tenet of a sound technical trading strategy is to study the character of the consolidation or reversal when a broad move pauses. A healthy consolidation, whereby longer-term investors replace shorter-term traders, can be seen through a methodical "backing and filling" (or a pattern that looks like a staircase with a rise higher followed by a small retreat). It is through this consolidation that various stocks begin to develop new bullish patterns, offering new trading opportunities to the astute observer. Under this traditional premise, you might assume that 2009's 23% rise had its fair share of healthy pullbacks and subsequent bullish setups. However, this assumption based on basic technical analysis would be incorrect.

From the very beginning of the rise, it almost seemed as if the disbelief of the investing community was, in fact, the catalyst behind the rise itself. Although this is true in part for any reversal, where short covering provides the initial force behind higher prices, sustained moves higher are known to be followed by actual demand for stocks rather than bearish investors reversing their positions. It is at this time that institutions provide notable volume, scooping up select stocks becoming new market leaders and letting even the casual observers know that an advance is widely support-ed. Even though a wall of worry or a market that moves higher based on pessimism rather than optimism is a common, short-term investing theme, 2009 was much different. Not a single text I have ever read says that any sustained rally may come from a con-tinuous stream of pessimistic investors seeking to capitalize on a reversal, thereby setting the stage for repeated and continuous short squeezes higher. From my vantage point, this is what hap-pened throughout 2009. The ease with which retail investors could short stocks through inverse ETFs (exchange traded funds), in combination with the vast amount of traders who understand and attempted to apply basic technical analysis, along with the broad pessimism surrounding the economy, created an environment prone to short squeeze after short squeeze, sending the market higher with very few participating.

For example, you didn't have to be a technical analysis guru to be aware of the head and shoulders pattern that had developed on the S&P 500 around July of that year, shown in Figure 4.1. This historically bearish pattern, where the movement of a stock or market takes on the look from which it is named, received unprecedented attention in not only trading circles but also in the mainstream financial media. I would argue that this very notoriety was the primary reason the pattern was doomed to fail, simply because of the number of traders looking to play it. When the pat-tern didn't result in lower prices as traditional technical analysis would suggest, it set the stage for one of the biggest short squeezes in the history of the market, as shown in Figure 4.2.

**Figure 4.1** *In July 2009, the market had carved out one of the most widely discussed head and shoulder topping patterns in history.*

Chart courtesy of Worden—www.Worden.com.

**Figure 4.2** *In July 2009, the head and shoulders pattern failed to break down, resulting in a dramatic short covering rally higher.*

Chart courtesy of Worden—www.Worden.com.

From that point forward, not a single market drop looked like healthy consolidation from a traditional sense and was therefore embraced by the general trading world as the top. Opportunistic traders sought to capitalize on this, positioning on the short side only to be squeezed time and again. As the masses moved in to short, the trade quickly became overcrowded and did not work. As these traders reversed their positions, it resulted in an incredible move higher, altering the technical picture from looking rather bearish to new highs in the blink of an eye. This played out time and again to the point where a "bearish pattern, turned bullish break" became the norm. Although I didn't trade the pattern as often as I should have, one of the most successful long side trades of 2009 was buying what is traditionally called a bearish wedge, a pattern that would normally be shorted. True to its name, the bearish wedge is a consolidation pattern insinuating lower prices in the future. Bearish wedges were common in 2009 after a decline. However, because many investors attempted to capitalize on these patterns to the short side, the patterns no longer played out as they traditionally would. Instead of shorting these traditionally bearish patterns, the profitable trade became buying them, throwing conventional technical analysis out the window. It became so successful that traders jokingly dubbed the pattern the "bullish cliff," stating that the steeper the decline before the consolidation, the more leverage to use going long. It was humorous at the time, but little did we know how much foresight it actually contained.

To understand 2009, you must understand the general investor mindset leading up to that year. The incredible decline of 2008 led many on a quest to not just understand how to avoid such a drop but to profit from it. Few strategies, outside of technical analysis, protected traders from the bear market of 2008 while also allowing them to profit from it. When the decline was over and the damage done, the frustrated masses flocked to technical analysis, seeking to understand more about the strategy and use it to their advantage. Of course, once again, the crowd was simply setting themselves up for disappointment. The untold masses seeking to utilize basic technical analysis led to the direct opposite outcome from what most were hoping for. Time and again, these strategies failed in 2009. You would be wise to remember that when so many are utilizing the same strategy, it will rarely work.

In 2009, basic technical analysis was thrown out the window, and simply doing the opposite would have netted the investor a hefty profit. Can you then conclude that traditional technical analysis is dead, never to be successful again? I believe that conclusion is foolish. However, I will argue that the successful trader's strategy will account for the ever-changing landscape that is made up of other traders. Rather than being held to a specific set of rules or style, what we learn from 2009 is that you must be willing to adapt to what other traders are doing, seeking not just to capitalize on the market itself, but also on the actions of others you are trading against. Most will review the rise off the March 2009 bottom and simply conclude that next time they will buy into the weakness and hold longer, capitalizing on higher prices. If this is their only takeaway from 2009, most traders will completely miss some of the most important lessons presented. The real lesson is that you must not only observe the market, but you must also observe the market participants. When the masses have moved to using traditional methods, such as technical analysis, you must be willing to trade on the failure of these patterns to exploit the crowd's movement for your own benefit.

# chapter 5

# Finding Your Edge

Now that you have had a glimpse into the world of trading the trader, you must understand that before you can derive any edge from this, you must first have a viable and proven strategy in place. It is from this foundation that your versatile strategy will be supported.

Imagine, if you will, a trained chef entering your kitchen to whip up a quick dinner. With a firm knowledge of what seasonings or spices pair well, I suspect the chef could take whatever you happened to have on hand and cook an incredible meal. On the other hand, if I were to enter your kitchen with the task of making dinner, more than likely we'd be calling out for Chinese. Simply stated, I do not possess the foundational knowledge of what works well with what when it comes to cooking. Not only do I not know what pairs well, I am not familiar with most of the ingredients. If I were to consult anything more than a basic cookbook, I would have to also research the various ingredients along the way, to truly understand the instructions. Because of my limited knowledge, if my desire were to become a real chef or someone with a similar capability, the best place for me to start would be the basics. I would first have to develop a strong foundation from which I could build on over time. This is true in any profession, and trading is no different.

I am always amused when someone close to me suggests they are considering going into trading. Typically, this person hasn't a clue about the vast workings of the markets, but may have been intrigued by a commercial or other advertisement discussing just how easy it is to take control of their investments. In the past, I would genuinely point the novice to a few books, or suggest some other means of education. Now, I just invite them to my office to discuss their desire further. It rarely fails that when someone steps into my office, seeing the multiple computers, eight monitors, and access to such tools as real-time futures charts, global markets, and forex (foreign exchange), not to mention news from every source imaginable, all being piped in at a ridiculous speed, that a light bulb goes off, and the reality sinks in, that a person like me will be on the other side of their trades. It is only then that they realize this game is not man versus market, but trader versus trader. It doesn't mean that you must have sophisticated or robust equipment to succeed, but it does mean that you must understand the business, possess a proven strategy, and fully grasp whom it is you are trading against.

No shortcuts exist when embarking on the journey of becoming a successful and consistent trader. It is also dangerous for you to jump too far ahead, starting to analyze what other traders are doing without having a firm foundation already in place that can provide the footing for a flexible strategy. It would be easy for you to simply conclude that in a current environment all traders are buying stocks that are breaking out of consolidation patterns and therefore shorting those same stocks or betting against these traders may be the better play. In reality, this might be a time when what the masses are doing works very well and fading them is a lost cause. Rather than jump too far ahead less you become completely confused, let's first begin with your basic strategy.

If I were to ask you to write down your trading strategy, could you? If someone were to ask you how you buy and sell stocks, could you clearly articulate for them your detailed process? More than likely, you develop a detailed list before heading out to run errands. Or maybe you follow a strict regimen when approaching a large purchase, such as checking various websites or scanning periodicals for consumer feedback. Yet when it comes to investments or trading, you might follow no defined system that you are confident provides you the edge needed to profit. However, *having one is a must*.

At the core of every successful trader lies a defined trading strategy, which ultimately provides a statistical and proven edge. While you will refine your strategy over time, thus also improving your edge, your job is to execute this strategy over a large enough sample set of trades to be consistently successful. For example, let's assume that you have a proven strategy that yields you a slight edge, and over a large enough trading sample you may see 55% of your transactions as profitable trades. If this were the case, to be consistently successful you would just exercise your strategy, actually losing 45% of the time; yet because of the slight odds in your favor, you would still be profitable. For some reason, we're led to believe that to be successful traders we have to pick incredible stocks or take unbelievable amounts of risk. The reality is that you simply need a slight edge and the patience to exercise that edge over and over again.

In my experience of training numerous individuals over the years, I have often found that most developing traders lack a solid strategy and thus have no real foundation in place to build on. The first thing I typically ask people is to articulate the trading strategy that provides them their edge. Most of the time, I hear rambling answers that contain something about buying low and selling high. Such traders and I often spend the first several hours together defining a new strategy from the beginning and laying the initial bricks that will ultimately serve as the foundation for success.

I have read that upward of 90% of those attempting to trade stocks fail. I would actually argue that this number is much higher. The greatest paradox is that failure in trading does not at all correlate with a lack of proven strategies available for you. Countless strategies provide a proven statistical edge. The problem with most people, I believe, is that quite often the strategy selected does not mold well with their own unique personalities. Furthermore, traders often believe that a set strategy should work in all environments, when, in fact, the best traders alter their strategy to adjust to the environment they're in at the time. This continuous failure leads to the endless search for a new strategy, which ultimately creates more frustration and soon leads to yet another failure. The truth is that most people spend a lifetime searching out new trading strategies, on a cycle of continuous failure, whereas the successful trader spends a lifetime honing the strategy already consistent in bringing gains.

# Value Investing

The mother of all strategies known to traders is *value investing,* made most popular by the great Warren Buffett. This buy-and-hold strategy is typically taught in the academic world and traditionally passed through various generations. Although many traders debate the merits of this strategy, particularly during bear markets, there is no question that the strategy has proven successful for those who have mastered it. You might be able to argue against a buy-and-hold strategy for a random set of stocks over a given time period, but the argument that Warren Buffett has not been successful adhering to this strategy simply does not hold water.

I firmly believe that if you want to set off on this path, enough resources are available for you to become extremely successful. You can still find all of the late Benjamin Graham's material, the individual who taught Warren Buffett, and any number of other books on the subject.

You need to ask yourself one question when you approach a style such as this: Do I have the patience and the fortitude to wait for my analysis to come to fruition? I believe that although you might want to invest like Warren Buffet, you will not stomach watching your nest egg decline by tremendous amounts in the short term as you wait for your analysis to be proven right by the market in the long term. When asked about a declining investment such as Coca Cola (KO), a stock Warren Buffett has owned for decades, he traditionally states that he cares not where the stock price is but rather how the business is doing. He argues that you should never act as if you own shares of stock but instead act as though you own the entire business. Although this might work well for him, most traders cannot sit through the incredible ups and downs in price over the years. It is a sound strategy, but it might not suit your personality.

While reviewing the performance in 2008, I read up on some of the most notable value investors of our time. It was not uncommon to see negative 60% and 70% returns during a time of terrible market performance. I have no doubt that most of these investors will do extremely well over the next decade and make back their unrealized losses and much more. However, you must honestly ask yourself whether you could handle such a decline. Typically, that answer is no, yet value-based investing remains one of the most popular and widely accepted strategies around. If you set off down this path, yet cannot accept the drawdowns in your account, you are once again destined for failure.

# Day Trading

Despite being shunned by the general public as a credible way in which to approach the market, day trading is one of the most efficient and successful ways in which to make consistent profits. Most of the successful traders I know, while they may follow a different strategy to select and manage their trades, share a common bond in that they go to cash each and every night before closing up for the day and are therefore deemed *day traders*. Their goal is to possess no overnight risk whatsoever, coming into each day with a clean slate, an open mind, and the willingness to deploy capital as their strategy dictates in either direction depending on what the market presents them.

I have great experience with day trading, and I can tell you the exhilaration and freedom from day trading is fantastic. Markets have become increasingly volatile, and to see the market shift in an extremely short time period is not uncommon. A day trader has the unique advantage of playing the day's move regardless of whether that move correlates with the previous day's move. In contrast, if you come into the day holding positions, you will already be biased as to the direction you desire. Holding positions over night means that you are more than likely positioned for the previous day's trend, when the next day may be different.

On the surface, the life of a day trader looks attractive, and I suspect that is one of the reasons so many traders are initially drawn to the style. However, more often than not, most learn that day trading is not for them and is an unrealistic venture for them to pursue (because of their schedules, their temperament, or perhaps a combination of both). Furthermore, you might make the classic mistake of believing that day trading is the actual strategy, when in reality day trading is merely a general term that means an individual ends the day with no positions. Within this general style lie hundreds if not thousands of different strategies. Individuals often believe that day trading may be the style for them and move head long into this world without having a set strategy to follow, once again setting themselves up for failure.

It reminds me of someone driving along on a nice sunny day and noticing a jogger out for a run. The driver thinks to himself how nice it would be to be back in shape, outdoors, enjoying a run on a beautiful day. When he returns home, he puts on the old tennis shoes, throws on the shorts, and heads out for a run. Within a block or two, he is reminded of the harsh reality that running isn't as easy as it looks and that he is incredibly out of shape. When watching the runner strutting along, the driver failed to see the countless hours that the runner had been training. He didn't see the early mornings, the runs in the rain, the cold, or the early days when just running a mile or two was exhausting. He saw the end result, appreciated the beauty of it, and wanted to skip all the work and enjoy the prize. Clearly that isn't going to happen in running, and it won't happen in trading.

Most people who observe a day trader, or start to study the craft, set themselves up for immediate failure because they do not properly assess their own personality, much less their own schedule, before determining whether day trading is even an option for them. At its most basic, day trading generally requires an incredibly demanding schedule. To capitalize on the opportunities presented on any given day, you must be able to sit at your computer throughout the entire trading day. Unfortunately, you cannot dictate when the great opportunities will come. Instead, you are at the mercy of when the market wants to make these opportunities available. Although this might be a reality for some, odds are that you may have other obligations throughout the day to attend to that do not allow you to sit and monitor markets each and every day, all day long. Furthermore, like myself, some people just don't enjoy being tied to the computer and positions all day long. As I mature through adulthood, I have begun to once again appreciate stepping outside during the day, enjoying lunch with friends and family or the occasional vacation. I do dabble with a day trade here and there, but I much prefer to see a position work for me over time, not a trade mandating I watch its every tick.

As stated previously, don't be confused by assuming that day trading is a strategy within itself. It is not. You cannot just adopt the term *day trading* to supplement your lack of a solid trading strategy. Once a strategy has been put in place, you might decide to day trade that strategy. However, the time frame does not come before the strategy. Day trading is a world within itself that comprises many different strategies, most of which do share a common bond with our next general category, the world of technical analysis.

# Technical Analysis

Unlike its counterpart fundamental analysis, technical analysis is not traditionally passed on from generation to generation, nor is it taught at the academic level as a method of successful investing. In fact, technical analysis often receives negative press despite the fact that the foundation of technical analysis, a chart, is used to display a stock's movement on almost every media outlet that discusses investment information. Many of the same people who refuse to respect technical analysis will actually talk about uptrends, support, and resistance. It's really quite humorous.

Although the popularity of technical analysis has grown to unprecedented levels, and therefore has become quite saturated, it remains one of the best investment methods for you to follow when developing your own personal investment strategy. Like the world of fundamental value investing, technical analysis may be broken into several categories with a primary principal woven throughout. The common principal is the adherence to quantifiable evidence shown through historical price and volume, allowing you to infer where a stock may move next. Based on my experience, the best way to describe technical analysis to a novice is by explaining that charts graphically represent other traders' emotions. I explain how historical price, which is directly tied to the emotions of other traders, enables you to find key inflection points whereby a move may begin or end. After these inflection points have been determined, you can then position your capital accordingly (in your attempt to profit).

The world of technical analysis is vast in that the individual strategies within the general investment methodology are too numerous to mention within the scope of this book. I have seen technical traders find their edge mastering such indicators as trend lines, moving averages, pivot points, stochastics, relative strength, and Fibonacci numbers. To assume that one method is superior to another is arrogance. Over the years, I have learned to greatly respect most individual strategies within the world of technical analysis. This respect has not come blindly. It has come over many years from directly witnessing traders gaining an edge via these methods.

Over the past decade, markets have punished buy-and-hold investing, which encompasses many of the traditional investment styles widely taught and accepted. Therefore, basic technical analysis has boomed in popularity as traders seek yet another style that might be their ticket to riches. For the astute trader, this new popularity and shift toward technical analysis has created another layer of incredible opportunity. It is no longer enough just to follow the basics of technical analysis. Instead, the real edge now is trading the traders who are trading the basics. Never before has a "trade-the-trader" style incorporated into the foundation of an existing strategy been more important, or more lucrative. Unlike other styles of investing that may remain true forever, technical analysis must always be tweaked, because of the ever-changing landscape and mood of the trading world. However, never view this as insurmountable. Instead, accept this fact as one of the many routine challenges on the way to consistent profits. I have come to learn that embracing this is half the battle.

We have covered only a few brushstrokes here. Literally hundreds, if not thousands, of proven strategies exist from which you may choose to find your edge. These are proven strategies that traders at this very moment make consistent profits from year after year. However, despite the large number of strategies available, most people will continue to struggle and fail at trading, regardless of the relevant resources available to them. With so many successful and consistent strategies available, it raises the question as to why more people are not successful at trading stocks? I believe that even though the number of proven strategies is great, if you do not seek to master the strategy that fits your personality, temperament, and schedule, you are certainly doomed to fail. Adhering to a proven strategy that fits your personality is the foundation of successful investing.

Imagine, if you will, pursuing a passion for golf. You study professional players' swings, play hundreds of rounds, and ultimately seek professional help. Despite your best efforts, you still can't improve your score, and your frustration builds with every passing day. One day, however, you learn that there is an appropriate club length for each person and that you have been playing with clubs 6 inches too short. The short clubs never allowed you to have an adequate swing. In fact, they were slowly damaging your physical health, placing strain on your lower back and shoulders. Finally, you are fitted for the appropriate-sized clubs. Upon swinging the clubs, you immediately notice a world of difference. The clubs themselves do not immediately improve your score, but they no longer hinder the success you desire. Well, friend, if you are attempting to trade without a strategy that suits you, you are like the golfer with short clubs. You are doomed from the start and will never be in a position to prosper until you alter the basic foundational issues.

The truth is that most traders never truly subscribe to a specific strategy. Even if you do, it might not be the one that fits you best. Furthermore, you may desire a strategy to work consistently, on every given trade, when in reality this is impossible. You might not be willing to ride out the lean times (nor are you taught how to). Therefore, you might become frustrated with a strategy during one if its natural downtimes and abandon it altogether. Whether it is for a lack of a good fit, or a period of drawdown, the trader who ventures down this path mistakenly believes that it is the strategy that is at fault, when it is really the trader who is in the wrong. Once one strategy is abandoned, the trader moves on to the next strategy, ultimately repeating the process, and thus sparking the vicious cycle I call the endless strategy search.

Perhaps you are on the endless strategy search right now, and that is why you are reading this book. Those traders on the endless strategy search hop from book to book, website to website, trading service to trading service, trying to find that magic strategy that will make it all click. Although they might enjoy brief periods of success, failure always ensues, and frustration builds. The idea of abandoning stock trading altogether seeps in, yet they see others supposedly having success and so they refuse to give up until they have discovered the secret. Eventually, some either become skeptical of the stock trading community as a whole, never truly believing that anyone is really successfully trading stocks, or they go broke. A few lucky ones, those who make up the small percentage of those finding success, finally find a strategy right for them and ultimately learn the tools needed to succeed over the long term.

Your strategy is like the foundation of a house; it must be sturdily in place before other layers can be built on it. Furthermore, you must know it is successful (in that it gives you the edge needed to make consistent profits over time). So far, we have discussed various strategies and could discuss many others, but the purpose of this book is to walk you through a strategy that I have developed over the years and that has worked very well for me, and will work well for you. It might not be something you adopt completely, but it will set you on the proper path to developing your own unique and ultimately successful strategy.

# chapter 6

# Timing the Entry

Most people believe that the stock market represents what is taking place within the economy at that time. The successful trader, however, knows that this couldn't be further from the truth. It is this very misunderstanding that separates most people from their money. Although a firm grasp of the economy might assist you in formulating a thesis or a theme from which you may consider your investment options, we have already discussed the extreme importance of allowing price action alone to be your primary guide, rather than your own opinion on where the market should go. Throughout my career, I have seen countless extremely educated people lose fortunes in the market as they have bet in the direction of their economic opinions rather than with what the market is actually doing at that time. Unluckily, most of these investors end up being right as to their forecasts and market predictions. However, by the time the price action begins to confirm their economic opinion they have lost a tremendous amount of money or given up completely. Before going any further into this book, you must understand and accept the fact that the market can do anything at any time regardless of how irrational it may seem. Once you have truly embraced this, you can move on to the next step, which is to capitalize on this movement.

Whereas many traders apply their economic opinions to their market endeavors, many others seek out quantitative information to guide them in their investment selection process. Never before have you had such accessible information, from economic reports to fundamental research. With one click of the mouse, you can gather all publicly available information about a company: its financial status, projections, analyst research, and opinions about the future direction of a stock or market as a whole. Even if you have the time to sift through all the research available, rarely does this path provide a true market edge. In my experience, it is not enough to understand the inside and out of a publicly traded company or its prospects for future growth. You must also time the purchase correctly so that the price action correlates with your opinion of where it should go. The timing of the purchase may be the most crucial element. Unfortunately, rarely does a person who understands the fundamental aspects of a company study this key part of the trade.

Let's assume for a moment that two traders have spent a considerable amount of time digesting all the information about a local publicly traded company: ABC Corp. Both investors come to the same conclusion that the company has incredible prospects for growth, which should translate into a much higher stock price. The stock and market as a whole has been trending lower of late, so both assume that the stock is of good value, at that time selling at $30 per share. Investor 1, believing that attempting to time the market is a futile endeavor, does not hesitate and places an order immediately to buy 100 shares of ABC Corp at the market. Investor 2 moves from a study of the fundamental aspects of the company to the technical movement of the stock, seeking to learn where the stock has traded in the past and whether, in fact, the stock is ready for a turn. Instead of just jumping in, Investor 2 wants to try to improve not only his purchase price but also the time he has to wait with his capital committed for the upward move to begin. Upon further investigation, Investor 2 believes that although the stock is fundamentally attractive at the $30 price, he sees no other evidence supporting a turn and that previous bottoms in the stock have come only after prolonged sideways action signaling the stock is done going down. Unlike Investor 1, who already purchased shares, Investor 2 waits patiently while the stock continues its slide. Investor 1 initially pays no attention to the continued decline in price of ABC Corp, reminding himself he will rarely purchase a stock at the exact bottom and it is his perseverance that will prevail. Investor 2 continues to wait patiently, stalking the stock's movement and attempting to time his purchase appropriately. After several weeks, the stock declines from $30 to $25 and starts to head toward $20. Despite Investor 1's research and fundamental belief about the stock's valuation, he starts to believe he was wrong in his evaluation. He thinks that by now the stock should have turned around. Investor 1 continues to devour all the information readily available to him but learns nothing more than he already knows. His frustration grows as he watches his investment decline. More time passes, and finally both investors recognize that ABC Corp has stopped going down. On one particular day, the stock hits a low of $18 and rapidly surges back to $21. After a long time of waiting patiently, this reversal gets Investor 2's attention, and he begins studying the stock even further on a daily basis. After some time, he realizes that the stock is now trading between $20 and $22, moving sideways in this range for several weeks. After this consistent back and forth, one day the stock breaks above $22, at which point Investor 2 immediately places his order for 100 shares. Over the next few weeks, the stock rallies 5 points, leveling off around $27 per share. After several months, the trade has so far shown Investor 1 a $3 (or 10%) loss, while Investor 2 has a $5 (or 23%) profit. Despite the vast difference in returns in the short term, some would hear that story and ask what the big deal was? If both investors desired to hold the stock for a significant amount of time, would an $8 difference in purchase price make that much difference? The short answer is a resounding yes, in that repeating this example several times over the course of both investors' careers adds up to a significant amount of capital. The emotional effect the exercise can have as a lasting effect on an investor's success rate is even more important, something we discuss in a later chapter.

Ultimately, the stock market is made up of human beings, and its movement is based on the cumulative emotions of all people participating. Although many variables may aid you in trading, the success rate of these trades can be increased substantially if you will also incorporate a study of price or the actual movement of the stock before committing capital to your idea. Furthermore, if you desire to set aside the outside qualitative variables, such as economic forecasts or fundamental prospects for the company or market, making a study of price and price alone, it is in my opinion that this is adequate enough to create a consistent and successful edge from which you may exploit and garner your profits. To study price, you must find a way to see the historical movement of a stock over time, in graphic form. Fortunately, like the plethora of fundamental information available at your fingertips, price can be seen through stock charts, which are just as easily accessible in a variety of places.

Charts have been used for centuries as a way to display a historical record of an index or stock's progression through time. Over the past several decades, stock charts have been increasingly used as investment tools. Despite their current ubiquity, I believe most people still do not truly understand how best to use a chart to give them an edge in making money.

To understand why a chart can provide any edge at all, we must first break down the basic emotions tied to a stock purchase, and thus lay the foundation for analyzing stock charts. First, however, I must stress that just understanding this basic principal and attempting to apply a strategy based on it will not work. Understanding charts and applying technical analysis is not as simple as understanding the human emotion behind investing and attempting to exploit it.

People buy a stock for any number of reasons. The previous example discussed two investors who pursued their own fundamental due diligence, but the simple fact is that most people either gather their stock ideas from others or they are directly connected in some way with the company in question. Perhaps you purchase a stock because it was recently written about favorably in a widely read publication. Or maybe a knowledgeable industry insider mentioned it on television. Perhaps you work for the company, did at one time, or know someone who does. Although the reasons behind the purchase may differ from person to person, the emotional cycle after the purchase has been made is typically the same. It is this emotional cycle that you must understand if you're going to seek to capitalize in the market based on price.

Let's consider another example. For whatever reason, suppose you decide to buy a local packaging company stock: XYZ Corp. You have had an electronic trading account for years that you use occasionally to dabble in stock trading. So, with one easy electronic click, you buy 100 shares of XYZ at $40 per share. The purchase is new and exciting, and so for next several days you check your account continually, looking to see how XYZ Corp is doing. You immediately show a profit as the stock climbs from $40 to $41 and then to $42. You wonder why everyone is always so caught up with how hard the markets are, when clearly you have a knack for picking stocks. You do a quick calculation in your head: If the stock advances just $1 per week, you will easily double your money over the course of one year. You go so far as to wonder what it would be like to be a full-time trader, leaving your mundane work for the exciting life and easy money of trading. A few weeks later when you are checking your account, you see that XYZ Corp has had a slight correction. After climbing as high as $43.50, is now back to your purchase price of $40. You shake it off, telling yourself that your patience will prevail and successful trading is all about riding out the ups and downs. You are a bit frustrated by having given back your $350 in phantom profits; after all, you had already spent the money in your mind. You quickly make the decision that when the stock reaches that level again, you'll cash out for a quick $3.50 gain, or $350, and call this trade a success. The following day, you check your account and are floored to see that the price has continued to drop from $40 and is now trading at $38.50. While you're quite annoyed now that your stock is showing a loss, you again chalk it up to normal market movement and let it be. You do, however, do a bit research into why the stock is trading lower and read a few news stories about the stock (after never having done so before). This new knowledge of why the stock dropped helps you to justify your hold. As the days go by, the stock slowly drifts lower and lower. One day, you check your account to find that your once $4,000 investment is now worth $3,000 (because the stock has dropped $10). Your frustration builds as you start to believe the game is rigged and you were duped. You hastily decide to sell the stock when it returns to your original investment amount. You remind yourself that time is on your side and you can wait patiently for the $30 stock to return to $40, at which time you'll promptly cash out and stay away from this ridiculous game of trading forever. As weeks stretch into months, the XYZ Corp stock continues to drift lower and lower. It is now that you might choose one of the many paths available to you and chosen by so many others in your situation. After months of languishing returns, frustration may lead to such discouragement that you just want to rid yourself of this stock and sell for a significant loss. Although that might seem logical, and is the case so often for so many, it has been my experience that most individuals hold on to the stock forever, whether it returns to its once famed price level or not.

I am always shocked to see stocks that will never return to the price at which they were purchased still held within portfolios. At some point, a stock's decline becomes so great that some people prefer to accept the entire loss rather than sell the stock to recoup the dwindled capital amount. I call these *portfolio graveyards;* the stocks held are dead and will never again return to life. You might be able to identify with this, and perhaps you have a few graveyard picks still in your portfolio. After you read through this material, however, I hope that will never again be the case.

The purpose of the preceding scenario is not just to relay the psychological journey of an amateur stock operator. It is also intended to show you how a chart can help define your edge. Knowing where a mass of traders is within the emotional cycle of a trade is critical information. Readily understanding this information would be nearly impossible without charts, which in many instances are free.

In our example, the stock never did return to the original purchase price. Had it done so, odds are you would have sold out for even money to rid yourself of the trade. It is this emotional connection to price that is the basic foundation for all technical analysis. The key to remember is this: Each significant price point that you experienced correlates to an emotional response shared by many others. Therefore, recognizing and understanding these areas of critical emotion on a chart may provide you the edge necessary for future profits.

Suppose, for a moment, that you originally learned of XYZ Corp in a national magazine outlining the top ten small companies in the United States. Or maybe you heard about the company from an analyst interviewed on television. However you learned of XYZ Corp, odds are that many others did, too. You can safely assume that after digesting the same information, many acted as you did and is why the stock showed an initial profit. If you are our base case, but also a good representation of a larger group of traders, your key price points assume even more significance going forward.

At this point, you might be wondering whether it is realistic to assume that people may act in harmony without knowing about each other's transaction. Yes, it is. The common thread among all those investors is that they are human and will experience similar emotions as the price moves accordingly. Some will argue that financial status differs significantly across the spectrum, and that more affluent investors will be less psychologically impacted by price moves. I would argue that an investor generally purchases an amount of stock relative to portfolio size and net worth, thus leveling the emotional playing field. Whereas $1,000 might mean nothing to Billy Bigshot, he may in fact have purchased 1,000 shares and therefore be experiencing a $10,000 loss. The key is to understand that average investors follow a path similar to our example more times than not. This cycle allows the astute observer to gather information about key levels from which to then garner an edge to support trading decisions.

The preceding example highlights the emotional roller coaster that creates the key prices that hold significant meaning for a particular stock, which you can see when analyzing a chart. Technical analysis as a strategy begins with the chart itself, instead of starting with a look at how the chart was developed. Ultimately, it matters not how these inflection points were created, only that we find a way to act on these emotional price points and use them to our advantage. In the beginning, your job is to interpret and exploit these inflection points for profit. This is the basic foundation of technical analysis, which has become the common pursuit of so many. Once you've mastered this, you may move on to the next level and actually trade the traders who are just trading the basics. At this new level, you suddenly have a world of opportunity unavailable to most others.

# chapter 7

# Trend Lines

Once you understand that you can use charts as a graphical representation of human emotion, pattern recognition is the tool that will enable you to begin capitalizing on the opportunities that present themselves on a daily basis.

Charts are readily available for all to see and use. Interpreting and using these charts is a different matter altogether. To the untrained eye, a stock chart is like a book to an illiterate person. It doesn't matter how big the words are printed or how basic the language. If the person has no comprehension or understanding of how to read, the book has no meaning. The information held within a single stock chart is so vast it is nearly impossible to unlock all the clues that a chart has to share about the potential of a stock or the general market. Attempting to decipher every bit of information is overkill. However, a basic understanding of charts can give you a significant edge in your pursuit of profits. When you begin to obtain profits by using basic pattern recognition, I believe you will embark on a lifelong quest to improve your chart-reading skills.

You might wonder whether traders trade according to technical patterns within charts because they lead to profits, or if technical patterns within charts lead to profits because traders trade them. The answer is both. You must accept the fact that sometimes a chart pattern develops because it is self-fulfilling and enough traders are expecting the same result. With most traders positioning for a move, it is sometimes forced to happen. As we'll discuss, however, my goal for you is to eventually find an edge within the self-fulfilling nature of many patterns that allows you to capitalize when the obvious pattern fails.

My pattern-recognition strategy can be divided into two primary categories: the lateral trend and the angular trend. At this point, you might be wondering about specific technical patterns that you've heard about and that have become popular over the years (e.g., cup and handle, head and shoulders, double bottom, and bearish wedge). Although increasing your knowledge about various patterns and the intricacies of each is important as you mature as a trader, within every famed pattern you can find lateral and angular trends from which you can make trading decisions. Consider, for example, the cup and handle pattern shown in Figure 7.1.

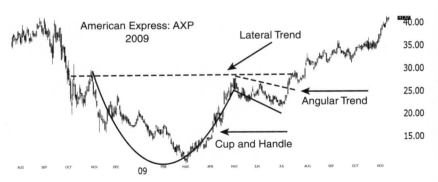

**Figure 7.1** *A traditional cup and handle pattern in American Express.*
Chart courtesy of Worden—www.Worden.com.

You can easily see where the cup and handle pattern derives its name. However, also plotted on the chart is the angular, descending trend line connecting the key points that make up the handle. In addition, I have plotted on the chart the lateral trend that connects the left and right side of the cup. You can observe the pattern as a whole, but you can also easily participate in a cup and handle break, by actually trading the descending or lateral trend line, as we'll discuss in Chapter 11, "Determining Entry Points."

The head and shoulders pattern is also mentioned quite often. You can see this pattern in the Goldman Sachs chart that Figure 7.2 shows. You can see the area that serves as the neckline for the head and shoulders pattern is also a clear lateral trend support line.

**Figure 7.2** *A traditional head and shoulders pattern in Goldman Sachs (GS) with lateral trend line support.*

Chart courtesy of Worden—www.Worden.com.

I have yet to find a popular pattern that doesn't have its foundation in either a lateral or angular trend, and therefore I do not spend time teaching specific patterns. Based on my experience, it's better to focus on the mechanics you can use to recognize and profit from the foundational trend lines instead of getting caught up in the multitude of specific patterns that exist today. There is also a dangerous tendency when reviewing named patterns to become somewhat blind to other possibilities. Let's suppose you stumble on a cup and handle chart with the intention of playing only the pivot break above the handle's highest point, the traditional execution for a cup and handle pattern. Observing only the named pattern, you may miss completely the ascending trend line that connects the lowest point of the cup and the lowest point of the handle and therefore not act on an ascending trend break down should this occur. You can see an example of this in Figure 7.3, the same American Express chart shown earlier in this chapter.

**Figure 7.3** *A traditional cup and handle pattern in American Express with an ascending angular trend.*

Chart courtesy of Worden—www.Worden.com.

When you embark on the pattern-recognition strategy, it is easy to become overwhelmed and make trading much too complicated. In the beginning, you must start with the basics, similar to a batter who spends time in a batting cage or a golfer on a driving range. One of the best exercises to begin your foray into pattern recognition is to identify and observe lateral trends. A lateral trend means that you can draw a horizontal line on a stock chart, connecting at minimum two high or low points, thereby creating a line that graphically becomes the lateral trend. Figure 7.4 is a daily chart of Apple Inc. (AAPL) in March 2009 that reflects a basic lateral trend line. At this point, do not infer anything from this chart. It is shown here just so that you can see what a lateral trend line looks like. Notice how the two highs can be connected to form a line. You can extend this line out into the future so that it becomes your lateral trend line.

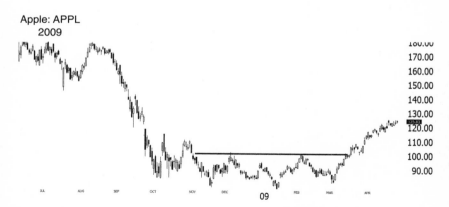

**Figure 7.4** *A lateral trend line connecting two points in Apple Inc.*
Chart courtesy of Worden—www.Worden.com.

In Chapter 6, "Timing the Entry," I discussed how investors become emotionally attached to a specific price point. This emotional attachment creates an *inflection point* for the stock, a price at which an emotional connection exists that favors a substantial increase in volatility, once the stock trades at or near this key level. Initially, it might be a news event or some other catalyst that sparks the key reversal creating the first significant point. If the news was negative and the stock dropped significantly, many traders might resolve to sell once the stock recovers or returns to the level from which the weakness first set in. When the stock makes its way back to this first inflection point, traders who might have been waiting to sell will do so, thus exiting the game and sparking another reversal at or near the original level.

The second time our key inflection point comes into play, it is still primarily driven by the human emotions tied to this level rather than other traders trading the pattern being developed. The reason for that is it takes at least two inflection points to create a trend line. If the second inflection point is still in question, it is only an assumption by the trader who thinks this level will in fact prove significant. This is a dangerous assumption and one reason I rarely involve myself in a pattern before an identifiable trend (with two or more inflection points) is first developed. Once the trend is identified for all to see, the pattern quickly moves from one being controlled by traders originally involved to a pattern being traded by traders who have identified the key level in play. At this point, the trend line in question usually becomes self-fulfilling as you and other traders cue in on this level as a natural turning point for the stock. Should this inflection point be above where a stock is currently trading, it might act as a ceiling or resistance for the stock. Should this inflection point be below, it could easily act as a floor or support for the stock.

As more time goes by, these points take on greater significance as more and more traders can see them developing clearly. As more traders become involved with the key level in play, once this level is breached, the stock has the potential to begin a very large move as traders scramble to reverse their positions and new inflection points for the stock begin to evolve.

Figure 7.5 shows a lateral trend line acting as resistance on the chart of IBM from August 2009. You can see that a line has been drawn connecting the peaks and thereby creating a natural ceiling for the stock over a certain period of time. Each time the stock returns to this level, it is sent back down as the level acts as overhead resistance.

**Figure 7.5** *A lateral trend line acting as resistance for IBM.*

Chart courtesy of Worden—www.Worden.com.

Just as multiple points from which a stock declined may create a lateral resistance trend, as Figure 7.5 illustrates, multiple support points from which a stock reversed upward may create a lateral support trend line. Figure 7.6 is the same Goldman Sachs chart shown earlier.

**Figure 7.6** *A lateral trend line acting as support for Goldman Sachs.*

Chart courtesy of Worden—www.Worden.com.

One common problem with traders who study technical analysis is that they never take the time to truly understand why it works, and so they sometimes get a bit lost in the minutia of technical patterns. Take, for instance, the preceding exercise. You will rarely be able to plot a flawless lateral trend line because rarely will a stock reverse at exactly the same price two or more consecutive times and thus allow you to plot this line perfectly. The stock will often reverse very close to the first level, but not precisely, before reversing. Or it might move above or below, albeit slightly, before turning around. Pondering the rationale behind the lateral trend, you should understand that the price point is of more significance

## EXERCISE

A basic exercise you can perform is to compile a current list of the NASDAQ 100 stocks. With that list in hand, visit any basic financial website that allows you to see a chart of a stock. At the time of this writing, I prefer FreeStockCharts.com, where you can set up the NASDAQ 100 within the left side bar and quickly and easily go through each name. Make sure the chart shows a daily time frame going back at least 12 months. One by one, input the symbol from your list, going through each individual name and seeking out lateral trend lines worthy of your attention. When you recognize one, write these symbols down on another ledger, along with the price at which the lateral trend line exists. If the program you are using to review the charts enables you to, physically draw this trend line across these points or print out the chart and with a ruler and pencil connect these key inflection points, making this line visible. It is important that you not only recognize the price at which the trend line exists but that you also see the trend line itself. At this time, there is no need to act on this from a trading perspective. Instead, just begin to recognize these lateral trend lines and thus begin your pattern-recognition education. Also note that you don't care *why* a certain level has become significant. It makes little difference why the inflection points have been created. Rather, you need be concerned only with the movement of the stock at or near this level. Place these charts aside and review them periodically to see where the stock is trading in relation to the lateral trend line you have identified. Incorporate into your daily schedule some chart time to do this. Just as an athlete practices during the off-season and between games, a trader's personal chart time is mandatory for consistent success.

earlier in the lateral trend's history than it is later on. The reason for this is the same reason the lateral trend is created in the first place: The earlier the lateral trend is within its development, the more human emotion is present. Once the lateral trend has matured and the stock has returned to the key price point on more than two occasions, other traders have become involved and are trying to profit from the pattern.

Suppose, for example, that a stock reaches the $30 level and reverses, heading sharply lower. The $30 level becomes the point at which shareholders started to lose money regardless of whether they bought here or had unrealized profits, which is what connects this level emotionally with those holding the stock. Eventually, after a drop, the stock slowly recovers and returns very close to the $30 level. At this time, those who have been holding the stock sell because they feel relieved to have at least gotten back to where they were before the surprise drop. When the stock declines for the second time from this $30 level, it becomes clear that this level is now of significant technical importance and more traders than just those initially involved will be drawn to this company name, seeking to deploy whatever strategy they prefer, around this key level. It is at this point that the general area becomes more important than the specific price. As the stock returns to that general area of support or resistance, more and more traders become involved. It should no longer be viewed as an exact level but rather a general level from which we can gauge the stock's next move.

Before I discuss how to utilize the lateral trend for profit, we need to review the second basic category of pattern recognition: the angular trend.

The angular trend can be divided into two segments depending on the direction of the angle, ascending or descending. Like the lateral trend, the angular trend can act as both a support or a resistance level and can therefore be used as a trading edge in either direction. Unlike a lateral trend, which typically marks a stock that has been moving sideways, the angular trend can be seen on a stock chart that has been increasing or decreasing in price over a set period of time. Figure 7.7 shows a basic outline of an ascending trend.

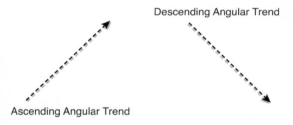

Descending Angular Trend

Ascending Angular Trend

**Figure 7.7** *A basic representation of an ascending and descending angular trend.*

Much like lateral trends, an angular trend first begins with a key inflection point, sparked by an unknown catalyst. Let's assume for a moment that a stock has been on a steady descent for some time because the general market has been weak and the prospects for growth for this company have been waning. When the stock reaches a new all-time low of around $10 per share, the company announces a new product that should boost revenues significantly and revive the company's stagnant brand. In only a few trading sessions, the stock shoots up 15%, moving from $10 to $11.50. You should have no anxiety over missing the initial move. Instead, you wait patiently for the appropriate point of entry, which will come once the angular, ascending trend has developed and been confirmed. When the initial move in the stock wanes, the stock should begin to digest the recent gains, possibly falling back to the $10.75 level. If the stock were to follow the development of a lateral rather than ascending trend, it might very well fall all the way back to the $10 level. However, in this example, that is not the case. For whatever reason, something that is irrelevant to you the technical trader, the stock does not retrace its entire 15% move. Instead, after coming back toward the $10.75 range, the stock turns up again and advances to $12. The recent advance creates what is called a *higher low,* and marks the second inflection point needed to create our ascending angular trend. For whatever reason, traders were not willing to wait for the stock to give back the entire move and instead decided to buy up shares on the first sign of weakness. Figure 7.8 shows IBM in January 2009 after an angular trend began to develop as noted. It is at this point, after the angular trend has been established, that you can seek to profit from the pattern.

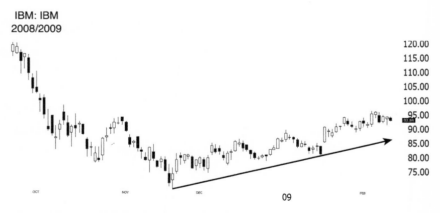

**Figure 7.8**  *An ascending angular trend in IBM.*

Chart courtesy of Worden—www.Worden.com.

Similar to the previously mentioned bullish scenario is the bearish case at which point a stock tops out and subsequently starts its decline. Through its descent, the stock develops a series of lower lows and lower highs, thus enabling you to draw a descending trend on the chart representing the stock in question.

In our bullish example, where the stock initially reversed at $10 and subsequently put in a higher low at $10.75, these two points became the basis for the angular ascending trend. If you were to connect those points but continue your ascending line farther on the chart, you would be plotting a potential path for the stock to move and logical support points for pullbacks. Once the trend is established, many traders might seek to act on this line as a guide, from either a speculative perspective or from a longer-term investing perspective. If you desire to slowly accumulate shares of this company, you may use this ascending trend for some time as a point from which to add shares, or for a shorter term speculative trade you might look to buy the dip and profit from any bounce off this line. After the trend has been established, traders actually playing the trend influence it much more than do initial traders who have an emotional tie to the price point.

Once you know how to recognize these trends, you must learn how they provide you an edge in trading. You can use these trend lines as guides toward profits in two basic ways. The first strategy is to go with the trend, assuming it will continue and seeking to profit by buying or selling at predetermined inflection points. The other strategy is to buy or sell a stock after a definite change in trend has occurred. Chapter 14, "Using and Controlling Risk to Your Advantage," discusses risk and trade management in detail. For now, however, we remain focused on the methodology behind capitalizing on the opportunities presented. Different market environments will typically favor one strategy over another, so it is important that you become proficient and comfortable in both trading with the trend and trading a break in the trend. This is challenging, which is why I recommend that you stick to just one discipline until you achieve a certain level of mastery and confidence. When you feel comfortable executing one strategy, you can explore the second strategy.

In conjunction with these strategies (going with the trend or trading a trend break), there are two methodologies of capital deployment: anticipatory and reactionary. Your schedule and available time usually dictates which one you choose. A passive trader might not be willing or able to sit in front of a computer all day and may be forced to take a position in anticipation of a bounce or break occurring. The reactionary trader will see the action unfolding and then act. I don't believe one methodology is superior to another, and that is why I never accept the excuse from those who say they just don't have the time to be a successful trader. Many of the most successful traders are rarely able to be in front of their computer on a weekly basis, let alone a daily basis. It is a myth that all successful traders sit in front of multiple screens with access to lightning-speed information and trade a gazillion shares every day. Although this is certainly the case in some instances, it is not a mandate for success.

While your own schedule and the amount of time you can spend in front of the computer during a market day may vary, what will always remain consistent among all trading strategies or capital deployment methodologies is the work involved in finding the patterns to trade. Unfortunately, this is just something that does not have a shortcut. Even though countless scanning products exist, there is simply no replacing the value gained when you take the time to go through hundreds of charts, not only stalking prey, but also gaining a feel and a perspective for what the market as a whole may be "saying." To consistently identify a strong list of opportunities, it is important that you develop a daily or weekly routine that includes chart work. Although they might not always be successful, you will at least be ready should an opportunity present itself. A great way to begin is by repeating the previous exercise, consistently going through the NASDAQ 100 time and again. Through this exercise, you will begin to see the patterns emerge and trend lines develop. You will see the character of the stock as it moves around a key inflection point, and you will begin to attune to the market and its movements.

Figures 7.9 through 7.13 display different trading strategies, along with different capital deployment methodologies, across

**Figure 7.9** *Fifth Third Bancorp breaks above a descending angular trend once acting as resistance.*

Chart courtesy of Worden—www.Worden.com.

different time frames. Study these examples and use them for reference as you eventually pursue your own opportunities in the future.

In late 2009, Fifth Third Bancorp had been consolidating under an angular descending downtrend for several months. On January 7, the stock broke above this downtrend and proceeded to pursue a multimonth rise. An anticipatory trader could have taken this trade ahead of the break, setting a stop below the previous November lows, while a reactionary trader could have moved in when the stock broke and closed above this line. Each trader would have secured a hefty profit over the next several weeks as the stock advanced.

**Figure 7.10** *Potash breaks above a lateral trend line once acting as resistance.*
Chart courtesy of Worden—www.Worden.com.

In the early part of 2009, Potash had established a lateral trend going back to late 2008. The stock was not able to break this lateral trend until May 2009, when it moved approximately $10 from its initial break point. Once again, both the anticipatory and reactionary trader could have secured hefty profits on the trend break within a few short weeks. The stock did, however, revert back to its breakout level in June 2009, which would have stopped our disciplined traders and left them with at least partial profits on the trade.

**Figure 7.11** *Exxon Mobile breaks below an ascending angular trend once acting as support.*

Chart courtesy of Worden—www.Worden.com.

All throughout 2009, Exxon Mobile used an ascending angular trend for support, as noted in Figure 7.11. In January 2010, however, the stock broke below this line, falling almost 10% before its recovery.

**Figure 7.12** *Chesapeake Energy breaks below an ascending angular trend once acting as support.*

Chart courtesy of Worden—www.Worden.com.

Chesapeake Energy had already fallen a great deal from its all time highs in August 2008 prior to a relief rally that developed an ascending angular trend. In September 2008, the stock gapped below this line, never to see this area again. Observing the angular trend development, an anticipatory trader could have moved in with a short position ahead of the reversal, placing a stop above the previous July highs, while a reactionary trader could have moved in when the break occurred. Once the ascending trend line was violated, the stock suffered a considerable decline, which would have resulted in significant profits for each trader.

**Figure 7.13** *The NASDAQ 100 breaks below a multi-year ascending trend line once acting as support.*

Chart courtesy of Worden—www.Worden.com.

Many times, observing the weekly charts of the indices will be of great help as you evaluate the overall market health. Figure 7.13 displays the weekly chart of the NASDAQ 100 from its 2002 low through 2008. Once the index breached this line, the selling picked up significantly, signaling the end of a multiyear uptrend. If nothing else, this could have been used as a significant warning sign that a bear market was imminent and appropriate action could have been taken.

# chapter 8

# The Basics Are Not Enough

A foundational trading strategy consists of both the understanding of pattern recognition and the ability to exploit these patterns for profit. It is my goal that by the end of this book you will possess both. Although these two items are essential, these basic understandings are not enough, and so it is also my goal for you to learn when to alter this basic understanding to profit not only from the moves in the stocks but also from the moves of others. As you start down the trading road, you will quickly see that if you were to pursue just the basics, many times you would be a sitting duck, opening yourself up to losses from those who have already moved on to the next level of trading the trader.

For hundreds of years, people have studied crowd mentality when it comes to the markets. These studies usually always come back to focus on fear and greed, especially during times of great volatility. The masses are always assumed to be moving blindly about, with the common thread being their emotional attachment to the broad market movements, over which they have little or no control. Strategies have been developed to capitalize on these mass movements, yet I believe we're seeing a fundamental shift that mandates our trading must adapt to these changes, too. From my vantage point, the masses are no longer being led blindly about but are educating themselves to pursue at least some trading plan that gives them a better understanding of the market and its movement. If my assumption is correct, the basics that most people are gravitating toward may no longer produce the desired results. Considering that these basics were initially developed to exploit the masses, if these same people are now pursuing these strategies, how can they possibly provide the same edge?

At its core, technical analysis seeks to quantify and predict the movements of other traders, giving the applier of the technical analysis an edge. It is assumed that when you study technical analysis you are studying patterns being developed primarily by those not studying the same thing. Although this might have been true a few years ago, today the landscape has shifted dramatically. Instead of pursuing technical analysis with the assumption that the masses are not, I believe we must pursue technical analysis with the assumption that the masses are studying the same. It is only with this thought that we can look objectively and realize that at times, to be successful, we must trade the trader who is simply trading the basics.

For quite some time, technical traders had a strong edge just playing the basics. It was similar to two chess players competing but only one knew the rules or was well versed in the game. The match was no match at all because the player who had no real understanding moved blindly about losing game after game. Sure, that person might have gotten lucky a time or two, but over the long run the person lost consistently. Finally, the player without any real understanding got sick of losing and began to educate himself more about the game and basic strategy. Assuming now that both chess players have the same knowledge of the game, as well as the same understanding of basic strategy, who will win? The winner is usually the player who can think ahead of the other player. In chess, this can be several moves ahead. At some point, it will come to that in trading, too. However, for the time being, you need to ponder only what the next move will be and make your decisions accordingly.

Let me explain further.

Odds are, you are already familiar with some common technical analysis terms, such as *support* and *resistance*. Furthermore, you are probably already aware of technical patterns, such as the previously mentioned cup and handle and the head and shoulders. If you are not aware of any of this, while you may believe you are with the masses, you are actually behind the masses and need to catch up quickly. Let us assume for a moment that you understand basic technical analysis enough to decipher patterns as they develop on charts for key stocks or markets. Let's also assume that a pattern begins to develop that can be plainly seen and leads you to position accordingly for what should be the market's or a stock's typical outcome. Years ago, you might have been part of a small group taking the action you did. Rather than be subject to the random ups and downs of the market, you would take your cue from the action itself. Once a pattern developed that you recognized, you would move in accordingly seeking a desired result. Now, you find that rarely do the patterns you have learned work as expected. Rather than be one of the few, you are now one of the many, and thus significantly decreasing the probability the pattern works in your favor. If the landscape has shifted and now the vast majority of traders are positioning for the same outcome that should transpire, doesn't it make sense that the odds of this transpiring has been dramatically reduced?

As previously discussed in Chapter 4, "The Other Traders," this was clearly obvious during the summer of 2009 when the S&P 500 had established a head and shoulders topping pattern that received more attention than I have ever before seen a technical pattern receive. The consensus was that the market had topped out and was preparing to roll over. This was confirmed by a head and shoulders pattern so widely accepted that the pattern itself was doomed to fail. Figures 8.1 and 8.2 display this pattern and its outcome over the next several days.

After this now famous head and shoulders pattern failed, technical analysis received extremely negative press when pundits relayed to us all just how wrong the pattern in question resolved itself. I viewed the outcome as something quite different and was convinced more than ever that technical analysis had power beyond even my wildest expectations, as long as I embraced the next step of understanding.

**Figure 8.1**  *S&P 500 after forming a head and shoulders pattern in July 2009.*
Chart courtesy of Worden—www.Worden.com.

**Figure 8.2** *The S&P 500 rallied significantly once the head and shoulders pattern failed to break lower.*

Chart courtesy of Worden—www.Worden.com.

The problem for most investors is that their belief about what technical analysis is ends with the basics when it should, in fact, just begin there. If at its core technical analysis is the graphical representation of traders' emotions and now most of those traders are seeking to capitalize by using basic technical analysis, your goal is no longer to assume the basics will always work. Instead, you must sometimes be able to alter your strategy to trade the traders who are trading the basics.

It is important that this idea soaks in. I cannot stress enough how incredible the possibilities are for profit once you understand trading the trader as an edge within itself. Simply imagine if instead of waiting for the head and shoulders pattern noted in Figures 8.1 and 8.2 to resolve itself downward, you immediately went long on its failure.

In the past, large financial institutions or mutual funds often provided the technical analysis footprints you could follow to gain a general perspective for where the market or a stock was moving in the future. These funds didn't usually bother to cover their tracks; instead, they moved like an elephant through the woods, plowing over whatever stood in their path, leaving a trail for most to follow. Over the years as competition in the institutional world has grown, it behooves mutual funds to be as strategic as possible as they attempt to outperform their peers. One of the ways in which they have done this is by no longer being so brazen with their purchases or sales. Mutual funds now understand the growing world of technical analysis and have the ability to significantly improve their results by using their size to influence the patterns traders are playing. As the mutual fund world has become increasingly more competitive, in addition to other products such as ETFs (exchange traded funds) or retail brokerage firms competing over this money, these financial institutions have been forced to alter their strategies a great deal.

To assume these funds and their traders don't know what the average Joe is doing, seeing, or feeling is an ignorant mistake. Traders at these mutual funds now prey on the basics of technical analysis to execute a better price point regardless of whether they are buying or selling. Have you ever been stopped out of a stock at a predefined level only to see it roar back with a vengeance after stopping you out? Did you feel like a sitting duck or that someone might have known exactly where your stop was? Well, would you be upset to know that probably both were true?

Suppose, for example, that a mutual fund has its eye on stock XYZ and wants to own several hundred thousand shares. In the past, these funds might have just start buying shares day in and day out without regard to any hint of secrecy. The rapid rise in price accompanied by a significant increase in volume would make it apparent the stock was under institutional accumulation. Because of the increased competition today, traders at these firms are now well versed in technical analysis and pattern recognition, and they understand that most retail traders are now using these strategies for their edge. These institutional traders also have the money and power to create or break their own patterns. Odds are that on the rapid price decline, where you were stopped out only to see the stock reverse course immediately, an institution sold a significant number of shares at a key level where they knew basic stops would be placed. Once this level was breached and the stock fell swiftly, due to the large number of stop orders in place, they were able to reverse their position and buy those shares at a lower price and thus lower their total cost basis in the stock a great deal as they bought into the drop. Is that wrong or illegal? Not at all, it's just the reality that most institutions have already accepted that the landscape has changed and to compete they must also change.

Understanding a basic pattern recognition strategy is a must and lays a foundation you can build on. However, once you gain this understanding, you must quickly thereafter start to think one step ahead. Throughout this book, I first lay the foundation for a sound trading strategy with pattern recognition at its core. I then conclude with a discussion about how to evolve this strategy from the basic to the advanced. It is extremely important that you first master the basics. Only then can you start to trade the trader.

# chapter 9

# Pick Your Time Frame

In the world of mathematics, the word *fractal* describes a shape that can be subdivided into parts, each a smaller copy of the whole. One of the greatest qualities about the pattern-recognition strategy is that it is fractal, in that you can use it across a multitude of time frames. For instance, the reasons how or why lateral or angular trends apply to stock movement are true over the course of several hours, as well as over several days, weeks, months, and even years. Because of this fractal nature, pattern recognition is a strategy suitable for a variety of traders regardless of their available time during the trading day to actually trade stocks. Because inflection points gain significance through human emotion, this emotion is present and can be seen just as easily on a ten-minute chart as it can on a weekly chart. Of course, the size of the move and time it takes to play out will usually correlate with the time frame you are reviewing. For example, look at the American Express (AXP) chart that Figure 9.1 shows and verbally state what you see based on what you learned in the preceding chapter.

I suspect you said something about the ascending trend and maybe went into a bit more detail about how you would trade the potential break down or reversal at support. Would you be surprised if I told you this was a ten-minute chart over a series of three days? What this means is that each bar represents a ten-minute time frame rather than one day, as is commonly the case.

How about the Gilead Sciences (GILD) chart that Figure 9.2 shows? Take a look at this and again relay your thoughts as if I were sitting in a chair next to you right now.

Would you be surprised to learn that this chart is actually a weekly chart covering the past three years?

American Express: AXP

**Figure 9.1** *American Express after breaking an angular ascending trend.*
Chart courtesy of Worden—www.Worden.com.

Gilead Sciences: GILD

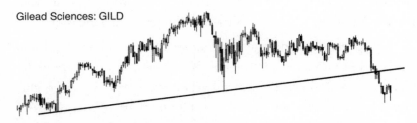

**Figure 9.2** *Gilead Sciences breaking an angular ascending trend.*
Chart courtesy of Worden—www.Worden.com.

One reason I never accept the excuse that someone does not have the time to become a successful trader is because of the fractal nature of pattern recognition. Sure, you might not have the time to trade ten-minute patterns, or maybe not even the time to trade daily patterns. However, if you want to be successful trading stocks and cannot review weekly charts sometime during the course of a month, you should probably avoid trading altogether. The good news is that with this strategy, a few hours per month can yield incredible results.

While the fractal nature of pattern recognition lends flexibility to traders with different schedules, it also opens the door for a common mistake among traders. Many traders never honestly assess their own schedules to gain a true understanding of how much time they can devote to trading. Without this finite understanding, it becomes a challenge to hone in on a time frame that suits you and the time you have to trade. What I will call *time frame jumping* can lead to frustration as you struggle to fit your personal schedule into the time frame you desire to trade, instead of adopting the appropriate time frame that fits your personal schedule.

Trading is all about knowing yourself. To be a truly successful trader, you need to look deep within, making a conscious decision to wrestle with those ugly qualities you don't want anyone to know about. If you do not do this, the market will seek out these qualities, prey on them, and use them to separate you from your capital. Maybe you struggle with emotions and tend to get caught up in the excitement when stocks are moving quickly. Out the window goes your discipline, and soon you are chasing names, filling up your position sheet with a long list of stocks that you aren't even sure why you bought in the first place just a few hours later. Or perhaps you wrestle with pride. Despite losing money time and time again, you still believe you know what the market should do. Rather than humbly approaching the market movement, willing to flow with whatever happens, you attempt to impose your beliefs on the market and force your strategy on the action. Although this might work for a season, it won't work for long, and you will quickly lose. Maybe you haven't truly reflected on your personality and how that correlates with your trading, or perhaps you are trading one time frame when in fact your schedule mandates you trade in another. A trading mentor and dear friend always encourages me with these words: "Be comfortable in your own skin." These words ring in my ears loudly, and I admonish you to take them to heart. Pause a moment and reflect on this a bit and how it applies to your own trading.

Before placing a single trade, you must firmly understand your schedule and how it influences the way you trade stocks. So often when I work with traders one on one, reviewing their previous trading records, I see a big disconnect between the trading world they desire to live in and the reality in which they actually live. When questioned about specific trades, they may discuss the pattern they saw that had evolved over the past day or two, or how a specific move in the market or other sectors sparked them to action. As they continue to tell me their stories, I see and hear strategies that would be suited for traders who can sit in front of the computer all day, capitalizing on the short-term fluctuations or swings in price or sector action. Even though the strategies are often sound, they don't quite fit with the life of business owners who in reality can sit at their computer only once or twice a day, checking the market for an hour or two at the most.

I'll never forget one of my boot campers, John, a dentist from Michigan, who struggled with this precise issue. John had an advantage over most investors in that his pattern-recognition skills were impeccable. He had become a student of chart reading and had approached the tape with the same precision as his successful dental practice and his scratch golf game. Despite these skills, however, he could not make consistent profits and was becoming discouraged by the endless downward spiral that seemed to plague his trading. As our dialogue increased before his visit, I assumed the issue would relate to his risk management or capital deployment. I thought that possibly John, like many in 2009, was getting too hung up on his opinions or a bias and was scared to deploy capital on the long side. Like approaching the market, I should have known better than to assume I understood what the issue was before spending significant time with him. I was pretty confident that even before he ever stepped foot on Kentucky soil, I had all the answers he needed. As we settled in during that first evening and discussed the past year, I quickly learned just how incorrect my assumptions were.

John talked to me about his daily routine. He told me that despite a full-time dentist practice he still put in many hours per day of chart work and market study. He followed along in my chat room and studied the stocks discussed there. His daily regimen produced a plethora of opportunities. However, when it was all said and done, his P&L did not reflect his skill level or work ethic at all. Despite his clear understanding of pattern recognition, John assumed he was missing something in his reading of the tape. John assumed that for him to become more consistently profitable he had to find better opportunities. Regardless of the fact that his initial assumption, like mine, was wrong, he possessed the humility to accept the fact that something had to change. He wasn't making money, and that was the only indicator he needed to know about.

As we spent hours discussing his trading, it became incredibly clear to me that the issue John was facing had nothing to do with mechanics. He could read the tape very well and knew how to check his emotions at the door. However, one glaring issue kept coming to light. With regard to moving in or out of a position, John often mentioned the short-term sentiment of the market or the short-term movement in his stock or another that led to his decision. When asked about a specific trade, he often said something like "I saw the ten-minute chart bottoming." Or "I played the real estate names because that day I saw financials turning green." It became clear to me that John was attempting to blend a very short-term strategy, or at least observe all the variables that would go into a short-term strategy, while in reality only being able to devote part of his day in front of the computer. You see, despite John's desire to sit and trade all day, his ongoing dental practice obligations kept him away from the screens for several hours. When he would return to the screen, he would catch just a glimpse of what was happening during that moment and would often make his decisions based on that information. Because the market often moves in a chaotic fashion in the short term, it was impossible for John to gain any sort of rhythm or sustain any momentum in his account if he was trying to trade on one time frame because he didn't really have the schedule to do so.

After recognizing this, it became clear to me that John did indeed have the potential to dramatically improve his returns but first needed to solidify his strategy much more. John had all the time in the world to study charts and find appropriate patterns. His schedule before and after market hours allowed him this luxury. However, when the market opened, he was distracted with other obligations. When he sat at his computer, he would make snap decisions based on short-term information that could change (often even between his patients). I strongly encouraged John to take a big step back and recognize that despite the allure, at this point in his life he did not have the schedule that allowed for short term trading. To be successful, he would have to focus his energy on a much more methodical approach, recognizing the opportunities presented in various patterns, taking them, and letting them play out. Furthermore, I encouraged him to avoid any "noise" that contradicted this strategy, shutting down the chat room and turning off the television if necessary.

To help John make this transition, we implemented some guidelines. John had lost a tremendous amount of confidence over the years, and it was important to rebuild this as quickly as possible. To do so, we had to reduce his portfolio risk, which meant that first we significantly reduced the capital John was trading so that he could become comfortable with his new strategy without being concerned about his entire account. Once he gained confidence for the time frame of his focus and had some "wins" under his belt, we increased the money he traded in a methodical fashion. We then limited the number of trades John could have at any one time to four. This kept John focused on selecting only the best four stocks. If another arrived that he thought had more merit, he would simply have to wait until either taking profits or it could replace one of his original four. Finally, we set a specific time frame that John would look at when selecting his trades. We banished the 5-, 10-, and 30-minute chart, and John could not delve into this short-term world. He needed to focus on the daily charts and thus give his trades much more time to play out (and not be shaken or distracted by the intraday movement). We concluded his rules by simply stating that once a position was taken, with a precise plan laid out from the onset, he would stick with that plan no matter what.

As is my custom, I follow up with all my students on a regular basis. John came to visit me in October 2009 and spent much of the end of 2009 reflecting on his experience with me and his new strategy. As of the first week in 2010, John had returned more than 3%, taking very limited risk, and was feeling more confident than ever. By the end of June, John was up over 10%, while the general market as measured by the S&P 500 was down close to 8%. An 18% outperformance halfway through the year is fantastic. John understands that there will be progress and there will be setbacks. However, I believe that John now has the requisite foundation in place, is comfortable in his own skin, and is making progress toward consistent success. John and I have since become great friends, and during a recent visit I smiled ear to ear as I heard his lovely wife talk about just how much their lifestyle had improved as a direct correlation to the reduction in frustration he experiences trading. Bravo John!

You might be under the impression that your trading time frame will somehow correlate with your returns. The excitement and faster pace of shorter-term price movement often insinuates greater opportunity for gain. I can understand how you may view those trading in this world and surmise that their returns should be exorbitant. It has been my personal experience, however, that this couldn't be further from the truth. Just as more opportunities for success are presented through shorter-term charts, so are the opportunities for failure, which can quickly alter your emotional capital if you experience a few losses in a matter of hours rather than days.

I remember vividly when it first all clicked for me. It was as if I were an artist finally finding my canvas. I understood pattern recognition and how to capitalize on the opportunities that were presenting themselves day in and day out. I had developed a way to calculate my risk ahead of my trade and had developed a profit-taking strategy that never let gains turn into losses. I saw firsthand how exercising my statistical edge over a sample set of trades produced a consistently rising equity curve. My excitement grew as I viewed my trading like I was the casino, with a small house edge, capitalizing on the never-ending supply of players that sit starry eyed at the blackjack table attempting to secure their future fortune. The house knows it may win some hands, it may lose some hands, but over the long haul its proven edge will bring in enough money to build lavish buildings and famous fountains. The system all made sense to me, and before long I concluded that to dramatically improve my returns and reach my maximum potential, like a vast casino floor, I had to be in as many trades as possible. Although the outcome I desired might have been possible statistically and is the foundation for many black-box computer strategies, I did not consider the human factor or my personal emotional makeup.

The day began, and it didn't take long for me to find my first few trades based off 30-minute chart patterns I had been studying over the past few days. I did not hesitate entering the trades, setting my stops as well as my profit-limit orders. Within the first 20 minutes, I had come across two oil and gas names that looked to be rolling over on the 5-minute charts. Again, I entered the trades and kept right on moving along. By 10:30, my daily alerts started to trigger, notifying me of longer-term trades I had been stalking for some time. I did not hesitate to enter those trades, too, adding even more inventory to the position sheet but remaining well in control of all that was going on. As I entered those specific trades based on the daily charts, my early trades on the 30-minute charts were stopped out for losses (while my 5-minute chart patterns played out and reached their first few profit levels quite quickly). While I was assessing the initial stop damage, taking some gains in the 5-minute chart patterns, I again had a few more alerts go off for charts based on ten-minute patterns. I scrambled to review those charts, while at the same time trying to manage my existing trades and review other daily alerts that started to trigger. While I booked early gains on the 5-minute chart patterns, the subsequent share amounts were stopped out and I was caught off guard when they reversed hard and created a little more slippage than I would have liked in the account. As the day wore on, I became more and more entrenched in the management of my own little casino floor. A few initial losses did more psychological damage than I expected, which had me hesitating on subsequent trades as they set up. When I began hesitating, I began missing opportunities.

It was the longest trading day of my life! When it was over, I had traded more that day than I had on any particular day in many years. The net return, while positive, wasn't nearly enough to justify the tremendous amount of work I had put in during the day. Furthermore, as I wrapped up the day, I stumbled on a few daily patterns I had missed throughout the day as my attention was focused elsewhere. This was rather discouraging because these patterns had evolved into what would have been outsized gains far greater than what I had made the whole entire day. In addition to all the frustration surrounding the actual execution and trade management of that day, I realized that my enjoyment level was far below normal. I couldn't put my finger on it. Some time later, I told a friend that the day was my first when trading felt like actual work. I subscribe to the idea "blessed is the man who cannot tell the difference between his work and his passion." That particular day was no fun at all.

My statistical edge is proven, and I still do believe that growing the sample set for my trading style would reap great returns. However, it is not something I desire to pursue. Rather than increase the size of the casino floor, I just want to hone in on the time frame and patterns that I find most comfortable. I want to strive for perfection within this world, and rather than increase the number of trades I enter, I want to increase the risk I take per trade. I accomplish the same end result without the manic activity.

The fact that pattern recognition may be applied across a number of time frames is both a blessing and a curse. You must first honestly assess the time you have to dedicate to trading, and thereby focus solely on the time frame that correlates with your personal strategy. When you have a firm grasp on pattern recognition as a strategy, and a core time frame from which to trade, you are ready to learn about actual trade management and the science behind consistent profitability.

# chapter 10

# Developing Your Plan

I'm going to assume we share the same understanding about the lucrative potential stock trading holds, and that you are seeking to implement a strategy that enables you to make consistent profits over time. What I do not know, however, is what your understanding is of the work ethic it takes to become successful within this field. I am consistently dumbfounded at the number of people who believe that with just a little work they can make consistent money trading stocks. It is true that the barriers to entry are extremely low, and almost anyone can open a trading account online and within minutes be in the game. However, to correlate the ease from which you can start trading stocks to the success you will have is a terrible mistake. You must know that the minute you sit in front of a computer screen studying the markets, you are facing not only the smartest people in the world, but the most competitive. You are facing ex-professional athletes who already know what it takes to succeed in the athletic arena. You are facing Ivy League scholars who calculate risk as if they were ordering a pizza. Finally, you are facing institutions that have an endless supply of capital from which to move markets, move stocks, and bounce you around like a Ping-Pong ball in the wind. After opening a trading account, like David facing Goliath, you are undermanned, underequipped, and the odds are significantly against your success. If you are not ready to commit the time and energy it takes to gain an edge against these challenging odds, do yourself a favor and find someone capable of managing your money with a proven track record of success in a variety of markets. If you have the drive, determination, and humility to learn, however, let's press on.

While I've made my frustration level for those who believe this is an easy game evident, I always must check this attitude at the door. It is these traders who think it's easy who will fall on the other side of your trades. Although equity trading is not always a zero sum game, those that do not understand or appreciate the work it takes to become successful do provide liquidity in the market, making your job and subsequent profits possible. I have been involved in many activities in my life, from athletics and academics to relationships and parenting. I can honestly say that stock trading trumps everything I have ever done when it comes to the work ethic needed to keep my edge. In my opinion, the stock market presents all participants with endless opportunity five days per week. However, only a small percentage of investors truly understand this and do the hard work required to become consistently successful. Are you ready to do the work needed to succeed?

"Plan your trade and trade your plan" is one of the oldest axioms passed among traders everywhere. Successful traders know that the less emotion they bring to the table when a trade is placed or being managed, the better off they will be. You are human and therefore possess emotions that can alter your actions, especially when you see your money increase and decrease before your eyes. Simply put, you must have already laid out what you should be doing ahead of time so that you do not make snap decisions on-the-fly.

Planning all the facets of your trade from the entry point, stop loss, risk taken, and exit strategy is as fundamental as the play called in a huddle for a football team.

Yes, a trader can be as free as a quarterback to call an audible, but the premise of planning ahead, before the action heats up, remains the same. Imagine a football team snapping the ball and the quarterback waiting until the defensive linebacker is running full steam at him before calling the play. I'm going to go out on a limb and say that the quarterback would be walking around with a few bumps and bruises after that game. This will not work during a football game, and it will not work during trading.

As someone who has made himself accessible to other traders and is always willing to help, I am often requested to diagnose various trading issues and investor styles. It is an experience I am always humbled by. However, over the years, I have now found that most conversations don't go any further than the initial dialogue. The reason for this is the first question I ask any trader I am working with: May I see your trading journal? This is not a trick question. After all, it is through written words I can better understand just what the trader was thinking before placing the trade. I can then see how the trader executed this plan and exactly what went wrong. As you can imagine, few who reach out to me actually have a written trading journal for their stocks, and therefore have no documentation to follow when they are in a trade. These are the traders attempting to call a play when the center has already snapped the ball. It just won't work.

I suspect most traders revert to a trading journal after they reach a certain level of frustration in their trading. My adoption of the journal-writing habit was similar but unique in that I had already been experiencing a level of success, but one that was far from consistent. As I began to review the only trading logs I had, my brokerage statements, I could tell very little about my actual trading strategy. It seemed easy to be a rearview mirror trader looking over buys and sells, cross-referencing those stocks to where they were months later, and surmising I just needed to either stay in a winning trade longer or cut a loser quicker. Regardless of how often I tried to implement such changes, however, it just never worked without a written record.

I subscribe to the belief expressed by Albert Einstein that the definition of insanity is doing the same thing over and over while expecting different results. Yet I also have learned that without the proper information, reflection, and study, simply altering the action might still not provide the desired result. Accordingly, each year I began reviewing trade record after trade record, coming away with the same realization: I sell too early. With a strong work ethic of reviewing a vast number of charts while playing favorable patterns, there aren't too many winning stocks I haven't invested in. Unfortunately, I stayed in those stocks for only a very short period (and they went on to mature into significant winners without me). As I reviewed this behavior of mine happening time and again, it seemed like an easy fix, with a logical adjustment of just holding on to winning stocks longer.

Each year, I made a new resolution to hold on to stocks that were acting well, longer. I wrote about this resolution, I discussed it with other traders, and like the early days of an exercise or diet plan, for the first few weeks I honored this resolution with incredible determination. Did it help me to start producing phenomenal returns? Nope, not even close. Time and again, the exercise mere-ly led to more frustration as I bent my rules, trying to stay in names that no longer were worthy of my capital, wondering whether this would be the one I would sell far too early. It was a vicious cycle for me, but one that I couldn't properly diagnose, not because I wasn't studying the trades, but because I wasn't studying the prop-er trading material.

I believe it was by accident that I first started a trading journal, but looking back, I'll call it a divine intervention. I remember counseling another trader who had reached a maximum frustration level to the point of quitting. I could see he had reached the tip-ping point, yet I couldn't let him give up the game he loved so much. MeatBaron, his Internet moniker due to his Canadian Butcher Shop business, had all the qualities needed to succeed: passion, humility, and a strong work ethic. Even so, he consistent-ly was being beaten down by the incredible volatility the market had been dishing out for a series of months.

Before he threw in the towel, I issued him a challenge, saying that before he took any trade, I wanted him to articulate to me exactly why he was taking the trade and that I might try to punch holes in his read. Furthermore, I told him that when he became confident in a read, could articulate the read well, and could also defend his reasoning after my interrogation, he would take the trade and watch it play out from beginning to end, regardless of the changing market, his opinion, or anything else that might alter his read. What the trader didn't know is that I had made a person-al resolution to take all the trades along with him, so that I too could experience the emotional roller coaster when real money was on the line. I wanted to get more into his head and learn where his brain went after the trade was executed, but I also wanted to have the stocks he was trading in front of me so that I could study them right along with him.

I suspect there was a bit of intimidation at first because for the next couple days MeatBaron was silent. It is not uncommon for me not to trade for several days at a time, but at this very moment there were trades to be had, so I guessed a fear of articulating his ideas was holding him back. He finally reached out to me, expressing his desire to take a particular trade that was setting up. He told me he had recognized a key level in the stock around a specific price point; we'll say $20, and the stock looked as if it were going to break above that level with unusually high volume. As I suspected, his read was not the problem, and the stock was, in fact, looking ripe for a significant move higher. I asked him where his stop would be and the various profit levels he was looking for. He answered without hesitation. As we were chatting online, I was copying parts of our conversation into another document, which ultimately became the format for my trading journal I use today. I also suspected I would need to use his exact words again in the future if he started to eventually doubt his read, the market, or the way in which the stock was acting. After some more discussion, we concluded that the trade was worthy of his capital. As I previously decided, I did not hesitate taking the trade and immediately bought an amount equal to the desired risk I was willing to accept on the trade. As the day concluded, the stock broke out and reached not only the first predetermined profit level but also the second. It was a very profitable trade within the first day, and with a raised stop level was certain to not turn into a loser. As I reviewed my notes from our previous conversation, I took the liberty of updating where the trade stood at the end of the day, and was amazed at my own lack of emotions over the trade, because I had simply been following a predetermined plan and not having to guess what my next move would be. A new world was opening for me, and I could tell this was the missing piece. I was also quite excited about the progression I believed MeatBaron had made that day, and reached out to him to discuss the day and the trade. "Excellent read," I said, as I began the conversation. "I went ahead and took the trade with you and was pleased to see both your first and second targets reached." I anxiously awaited his response because I believed we were well on our way. It took several minutes for the trader to respond, and when he finally did, he simply said, "I didn't take the trade." My heart sank. I asked what happened. MeatBaron simply relayed that he hesitated, and when it was time to commit his capital, he just couldn't pull the trigger. Regardless of how positive the exercise was, the trader I was working with had confidence issues that went far beyond what I initially thought. It took several more trades, and several more weeks, until the trader who consistently articulated to me excellent reads with excellent strategies was actually taking the trades he was laying out. We spent hours poring over our notes and reviewing trades. They were not all profitable, but eventually MeatBaron saw that he did in fact have a statistical edge, yet in the early going his confidence level had not allowed him to exploit this edge at all.

From that point forward, he and I both began our trading journals, and he has gone on to experience an incredible amount of success in trading. He knows that confidence no longer correlates with his profit and loss. His execution of his edge will bring him the profits he desires.

You *must* keep a trading journal for each and every trade you place for a number of reasons. First and foremost, your trading journal provides you with a road map you are going to follow when the actual trade is placed. With an ever-changing market, there are constant distractions and many changing variables, all vying for your attention after you are already in a trade. A trade journal helps you to stay focused on the trade you are in. When you feel there has been a change in the environment, or in your trade itself, you can review your initial thoughts via the trade journal to cross-reference. If nothing has changed with your initial read, your trade should remain. It is important for you to remain steadfast when you are in a trade and not allow the outside distractions to change your plan. This trading journal will also give you a paper trail or historic documentation that you can review to gain a better understanding of your strengths and weaknesses, and most important, to improve on your trading regardless of whether the trades were profitable.

It is of utmost importance that if you do not already keep a journal, you begin to do so at once. There is no grand format, and you may develop your own journal according to your own personality. However, a few key variables must be included regardless of whether this journal is kept electronically or in an actual binder. These variables are as follows and should be notated in the following order. At this point, don't concern yourself with the particulars of the list. We'll delve deeper into each aspect in subsequent chapters:

1. **Stock:** Simply notate the symbol so that it can be recalled at another time.

2. **Long or short:** It's easy to assume you will remember this basic variable, whether you are buying a stock long or selling a stock short. However, I always prefer to write it down so that my memory will be crystal clear.

3. **Stop and reasoning:** The point at which you would remove this position and why.

4. **Trade reason:** You should be able to clearly articulate why you are taking the trade. If you are following the pattern-recognition strategy, this should include a quantitative rationale and nothing qualitative, such as another person's recommendation or the feeling that a stock will act a certain way because of outside influences. It is this section where the more precise you can be in your reasoning, the better. Over time, and as you become more familiar with charts, this section will become much easier. I always tell my students to pretend they are telling me why they entered a specific trade. I encourage you to do the same. If you cannot do this, you should not take the trade.

5. **Risk per share:** The difference between your entry point and your stop. (You will usually enter this once the actual trade is placed.)

6. **Total risk for the trade:** Multiplying the number of shares you have taken by the risk per share will give you your total risk for the entire trade. This number should actually be determined well before any trade is placed, and will be the variable from which your share count is determined.

7. **Profit levels:** Calculating ahead of time where you will take profits is imperative to a successful trade plan. This allows the trader to remain focused on the objectives after the trade has actually been placed.

8. **Updates:** Any journal should also contain an update section in which you comment on the trade and relay anything you might be seeing or feeling while the trade is being managed. This section is critical for future growth as you recall what your emotions were at the time of the trade. In this section, you can update where and when the trade is ultimately closed and the gain or loss incurred.

The key to any trading journal is that it is implemented. Do not get hung up on the details at this stage. Instead, understand that your journal will evolve as you evolve as a trader. If you take this process seriously, however, you will have a written account of this evolution and be able to look back on this process and actually see the improvements taking place.

Keeping your trade journal current is not an easy task. However, you must consider that doing so is critical. You would never think of starting a business and not keeping accurate financial records to document your progress. As a business owner, you would most likely pore over these documents to both better understand where your business is and to better understand where it is going. You'd also want to learn from your mistakes, illuminate or reduce your weaknesses, and capitalize on your strengths. In the highly competitive world of stock trading, this is no different, and taking the time to document your progress is essential to your success. Not only should you rigorously document all your actions, you should also you review your trading journal on a consistent basis. I usually review my journal at the end of each day, with a longer review at the end of each month. By this evaluation, I can adjust my game to capitalize on the opportunities that are sure to be presented the next time I sit in front of the screens.

Regardless of how hard, how time-consuming, or how awkward it may seem, start your trading journal now!

# chapter 11

# Determining Entry Points

Now that you understand the pattern-recognition strategy and the importance of keeping a trade journal, we will begin to discuss and dissect the mechanics of an actual trade. In an earlier chapter, I briefly mentioned the two different methodologies I use when entering a trade: anticipatory or reactionary. This chapter covers each in detail, along with a hybrid method I call *delayed reactionary*. The examples included assume that you have already identified a potential trade and that the strategy of either going with the trend or playing a trend change has been predetermined. Let's look at a specific example.

Assume that through your daily chart work you have come across the chart of Ford Motor Co. on November 5, 2009, shown in Figure 11.1. You notice that the stock has been establishing a series of lower highs and lower lows for the past several weeks, developing a very notable angular descending trend line, which I have drawn on the chart. You also note that Ford seems to be consolidating in a tighter range, possibly preparing to break out of this trend and embark on a move higher. You suspect this because the market has been advancing as a whole, and the larger trend is clearly up. Therefore, you are inclined to look for potential longs. It is at this point you must decide whether you will enter this trade in anticipation of a break or act in a reactionary fashion after the break occurs. The methodologies are self-explanatory in that an anticipatory trade is one taken before the desired action, whereas a reactionary trade is one taken only after the desired action has taken place. Many variables come into play when deciding which methodology to apply, such as how confident you are of the pending action and how the general market is acting. The biggest variable, however, will typically come down to your trading schedule and the time available to be in front of the computer watching the action unfold.

**Figure 11.1**    *Ford trading below an angular descending trend.*
Chart courtesy of Worden—www.Worden.com.

Most part-time traders do not have the option due to their limited time, and so must use an anticipatory approach. However, this is not always the case. Although I do encourage part-time traders to gain a firm grasp of anticipatory trading, I have seen firsthand that one of the best methodologies utilized by a part-time trader is a reactionary style deployed in the final hours of the trading day. This method is the basis for the hybrid methodology we will discuss called delayed reactionary. Clearly, risks are involved with either, and each methodology requires its own unique variables, such as where to set a stop and how large a position to take. We cover these extremely important variables in subsequent chapters. I believe that as you evolve as a trader, you will eventually seek to perfect and utilize each methodology. However, in the beginning, it is of utmost importance to focus on one method at a time, to gain a fundamental understanding and experience a period of success before moving on.

Let's take the Ford trade a step further and dissect the different methodologies and review how you would have fared. Take a look at Figure 11.2. It is the same as Figure 11.1 except for the addition of an ascending angular trend and an arrow that notes the current consolidation. Because the stock is coiling up like a spring above and below two critical trends, you determine the probability for a significant move is high. You assume that the move may be a break up rather than down because the general market trend has been higher. You begin to study the stock, watching for signs to confirm your thoughts. As a passive trader, working your full-time job all throughout the day with limited opportunity to check the markets, you place a limit order with your broker to execute a buy at the $7.50 level, with a stop on a break below $7. (Do not analyze the stop at this time; we dissect stops in the next chapter.) The following day the order is executed as the stock makes a 4% move toward the upper trend line, closing the day dead into that key resistance point, the angular trend as noted in Figure 11.3.

The following day, the stock breaks the trend line and goes on to have a solid move, topping out in the very short term at $9.14. Assuming the broker executed your limit order to purchase the stock and you received a price around $7.60, the trade is already showing you an unrealized profit of 20.26% in the first two days.

It's at this point you might be shaking your head thinking that a 20% gain in two days is a rare event. In part, you may be correct. However, when you understand and can execute the pattern-recognition strategy, with a defined plan such as the one we're laying out, you will quickly learn it is not that uncommon to see incredible returns in short order.

**Figure 11.2** *Ford trading between angular trend lines.*

Chart courtesy of Worden—www.Worden.com.

**Figure 11.3** *Ford advancing towards the angular descending trend.*

Chart courtesy of Worden—www.Worden.com.

The difference lies within the pattern-recognition strategy itself that seeks to find trading opportunities prior to a bigger move. Most traders disregard the importance of proper timing, as we discussed in an earlier example of our two investors trading the same stock. In that scenario, Investor 1 did not seek to improve his entry point at all, whereas Investor 2 waited patiently for an ideal entry and thus improved his returns a great deal. As a trader, you should never accept dead money, continuing to hold a stock that isn't moving in the direction you desire. Furthermore, you should always be seeking to improve your timing and entering trades only when they're ripe for a move. There is a fine line between hyper-active trading based on impatience and allowing a trade to mature in a healthy manner, yet the purpose of adhering to a pattern-recognition strategy is to play the stocks that have the potential to move in a predetermined direction fairly quickly. Seeing rapid gains when you time an entry appropriately is something you will become accustomed to, and I suspect you will soon realize how powerful such a trading strategy can be.

Returning to our Ford example, let's assume that after recognizing the stock setup your schedule did not mandate you antici-pate the break. Instead, you could wait for the break to occur, before taking the trade at all. This reactionary strategy may improve the success rate of your trades, due to only entering after the desired movement has already begun. Assuming you are in front of your computer for most of the day, and have the luxury of waiting for the ideal entry to execute your order, it would make sense then, that you would not enter the trade at the same level you would have used when anticipating the break, but would instead execute at the price after the stock broke over the trend line indicated on the chart. For the purposes of this example, we'll assume that due to a normal delay, such as how quickly the stock was moving or how long it took to enter your order, you did not execute on the exact breakout price of $7.80 but rather $7.90.

Regardless of the strategy from which you entered Ford, the stock broke higher, showing gains for both the anticipatory and reactionary method. Because you were following the anticipatory strategy and entering before the break, the price from which the trade was executed was lower, resulting in a higher return on investment. Despite this higher rate of return, the anticipatory strategy was susceptible to the potential that the break higher never occurred at all. Because the reactionary strategy was contingent on the break higher to be executed, it made this potential for failure obsolete. Anticipatory traders often enter trades that never move according to plan. Why then would anyone take a trade in anticipation of a move rather than wait for the move to occur first? More often than not, the methodology you deploy will be determined by your schedule. You might not have a choice and will have to default to an anticipatory approach. If that is the case, you will have to be much more selective and exercise great discipline to find success. Make no mistake, however, that the reactionary style is far from foolproof. With so many traders seeking to capitalize on reactionary moves such as the one we've studied with Ford, many times these breakouts will reverse abruptly and result in a loss for reactionary traders in the same day. Typically, this activity becomes a theme dependent on the current trading environment and may be grounds to become a strategy within itself, whereby you actually look to profit from the failure of a technical break. Not only do you improve your odds of pattern success with the reactionary style by knowing the break has definitely taken place, but there is also the added benefit of a closer stop level. If you recall from our example, the reactionary method had a much smaller percentage stop than the anticipatory. This means you could take a larger amount of stock, while maintaining the same level of financial risk, as you did on the anticipatory trade. Stated further, if you were to enter the anticipatory trade at $7.60 with a stop below $7, you would be risking .60 per share. If you were to take the trade as a reaction to the break, entering the trade at $7.90, with a stop at $7.70, your risk per share would be .20. To expose yourself to the same amount of financial risk on the reactionary trade as you did on the anticipatory trade, you would need to take three times as many shares. Following my profit strategy, which is calculated using multiples of risk, you would achieve your profit levels much more quickly on the reactionary trade than you would on the anticipatory trade. Again, we will delve further into the intricacies of stops, risk, and profit levels in subsequent chapters.

Now let's take a look at what we'll call the delayed reactionary methodology. This is a hybrid of our reactionary style tweaked slightly to accommodate a more passive trader. Instead of taking the trade the moment the stock breaks the desired price point, you do not make a purchase until you are certain the break will hold. This generally means waiting until the trading day is coming to a close before executing an order. This hybrid methodology attempts to both improve the success rate of trades and to avoid same-day reversals (which are not uncommon) while maintaining the passive strategy typically mandatory for part time traders. This strategy does, however, assume you have the ability to check the market and your stocks within the final hour of the day to place any trades needed before the market closes.

For this example, let's assume you are checking back in on the market in the final hour of trading the day Ford is breaking out as shown in Figure 11.4. With the day coming to a close, you are certain that Ford has broken out. You did not enter the trade as it was occurring, nor will you wait until the following day to place your trade. Instead, you enter the trade at $8.15, a few pennies from the high of the day, which also happens to be the closing price. To ensure you do not remain long Ford in the event the stock reverses resulting in a failed breakout, you place a stop at the day low, which would negate the break of $7.75. As with our previous two examples, the delayed reactionary trade experiences a gain, as Ford moves higher the next few sessions toward its short-term top of $9.14. It isn't surprising that your unrealized gain for the trade while adhering to this style is smaller than that of the anticipatory or reactionary methods. Your financial risk per share is between both the anticipatory trader (.60) and the reactionary trader (.20), coming in at .40 per share ($8.15 – $7.75). In essence, you are willing to accept a lesser rate of return than was experienced with the anticipatory style to improve the odds that the initial break you are looking to capitalize on doesn't reverse the same day. The delayed reactionary style is a perfect hybrid for the part-time trader who still has intermittent access to his charts and brokerage platform throughout the day, specifically the final hour of trading.

Each style has its positives and negatives. However, only the anticipatory trade mandates entering the stock before the break, thus opening yourself up to the potential of the break never transpiring at all. You are rewarded for this risk with a much better return once the move unfolds (if and when it does). Once you understand the different methodologies, I suspect you will favor the reactionary or delayed reactionary style. For some, this just might not be possible. The anticipatory method is discussed and taught so that regardless of your schedule you can make successful trades.

**Figure 11.4** *Ford breaking above a descending angular trend.*
Chart courtesy of Worden—www.Worden.com.

The Ford example looked at a trend-change style using the three methodologies. Let's now review a trend-following style in which you seek to simply follow the existing move. Suppose, for instance, that during the early part of July 2009, July 10 to be exact, you stumble on Express Scripts. As noted in Figure 11.5, Express Scripts had started to advance off its March bottom, establishing a defined trend higher. When you found Express Scripts, you also noted that the stock was approaching the trend support or the area in which you would enter a long-side trade, buying the stock if you believed the trend would continue.

**Figure 11.5** *Express Scripts trading above an angular ascending trend.*
Chart courtesy of Worden—www.Worden.com.

Let's assume for a moment that you are about to embark on a business trip during which you will have little or no access to the Internet. Instead of passing on the trade completely, you place a "good till cancel buy limit order" for Express Scripts at $32, the approximate level you believed the trend support to be. This order says that you are willing to buy Express Scripts at $32, and it will remain an open order while you are away on your trip. You are willing to give the position some room to move, so you place a conditional stop order $1 below your entry, to be executed only if your initial buy order is placed and you do in fact own the stock at $32. As a side note, the broker you are using should have these capabilities and be willing to help you place the orders you need. Even if you don't fully understand the lingo, you should be able to explain your strategy and see your broker comply.

The very next day, while you are flying across the country enjoying your peanuts and in-flight movie, Express Scripts drifts lower, and your initial buy order is executed at $32. As soon as your buy order is complete, your stop order is also entered. The trade shows you a loss of .20 because the low for the day was $31.80.

However, this is still well above your predetermined stop price, and you remain in the trade. As the market continues to roll along, you spend the remainder of July taking care of your business engagements, while Express Scripts continues to follow its predetermined trend, showing you a solid gain of 15.63%, reaching a high of $37 on July 30, just 14 trading days after your initial buy order was executed.

In this example, because of your travels you had to be anticipatory or proactive with your selection and order entry. Let's now review what the trade would look like if you had the luxury of the stock confirming the bounce and trend-following pattern you previously laid out, before entering your trade. Not wanting to see a reversal the same day, you wait until the final minutes of the day Express Scripts bounces off the ascending trend, executing your buy order for $32.57, the closing price of Express Scripts. Because you don't want to be in the trade should it reverse and trade below your critical trend line support, you place a stop slightly below the day's low at $32.50. Without ever coming close to being stopped out, you experience the same move as your anticipatory trade, riding Express Scripts to a high of $37, just a few trading days later. The delayed reactionary method results in an unrealized gain of 13.6%. Although this return is below the anticipatory trade return of 15.63%, the financial risk for the delayed reactionary method was $.07 per share, whereas the anticipatory trade required $1 of risk per share. Let's assume the predetermined financial risk you are willing to take is a total of $100 on any given trade. On the anticipatory trade, you set a stop $1 below entry, which means you were able to buy 100 shares. On a delayed reactionary trade, however, by risking .07 per share, the same $100 risk allowed you to buy 1,428 shares. When the trade was all said and done, the risk reward was far greater on the reactionary side than on the anticipatory side.

Of course, not every trade will be profitable. In fact, as you become a successful trader, odds are you will experience almost as many losers as you do winners. It is only by exercising your proven and strategic edge that you will be allowed to consistently make money over time.

Let's review the different methodologies as we work through a trade that does not work and study its consequences. Let's assume that through your chart work you come across General Electric on February 1, 2010, as shown in Figure 11.6.

**Figure 11.6** *General Electric trading in between angular trends.*
Chart courtesy of Worden—www.Worden.com.

Despite the fact that the general market at that specific time was experiencing some weakness, your view of the longer-term trend being up, along with the bullish consolidation in General Electric, had you believing that a long side trade might be successful and worth an attempt. If you were trading in anticipation of the break above trend, you would waste no time, more than likely, taking your shares on the very day you noticed the setup. For the purpose of this example, we'll assume you execute your order at $16.25, the closing price for that day, with a stop at $15.50, risking .75 per share. The break you were anticipating doesn't take long to transpire, because the very next day the stock moved to a high of $16.95, edging out above the descending trend line shown on the chart. The day after that, General Electric did not follow through but rather reversed resulting in a failed breakout. Despite the reversal, your anticipatory trade is not yet stopped out. Instead, it shows an unrealized gain of 2.64%, or the difference between the $16.68 closing price on the day of the reversal and your anticipatory entry of $16.25. At this point, you might choose to raise your stop in the anticipatory trade, noting that something may be wrong with the trade if it did not follow through to the upside. For the purpose of this example, we'll assume you do not, because you are not able to review trades or charts (because you are once again traveling for business).

The following days, General Electric experiences significant weakness, not only reversing back to your anticipatory trade entry point, but far below, stopping you out at your predetermined stop point of $15.50 and solidifying a loss of .75 per share.

If you were not anticipating within General Electric, the reactionary or delayed reactionary style would have you waiting for confirmation of the break. Playing the reactionary style, you go long General Electric a day after finding the trade. The breakout level in General Electric corresponds to the highest trade of the day, so we'll assume you enter General Electric at the day's high of $16.95, placing a stop .20 below, the point at which you think the break would be a failure. Despite reversing slightly into the close, General Electric does not stop you out of your reactionary trade the same day, closing at $16.85. The very next day, however, you are stopped for your full loss of .20 per share.

Within the delayed reactionary style, you are waiting for a break confirmation in addition to making sure the break holds all throughout the day. Despite the small reversal into the close, General Electric holds its breakout level, so you enter the trade at the closing price of $16.85. Adhering to the same stop level as you would in your reactionary trade ($16.75), you use a .10 stop for your delayed reactionary style, which would negate the break and take you out of the trade. The following day you are stopped out of General Electric at a loss of .10 per share.

Let's assume that your financial risk per trade remained constant for each strategy you followed in the preceding example, and that risk was $100 for the entire trade. Because your risk per share was .75 within your anticipatory strategy, you would have taken approximately 133 shares ($100 / .75). Within your reactionary style, you risked .20, so you entered the trade by taking 500 shares ($100 / .20). Finally, within your delayed reactionary style, you risked .10 per share, so you entered the trade by taking 1,000 shares ($100 / .10). Because all three trades were stopped for their respective losses, each trade would have lost you $100, with only the anticipatory trade showing you a profit at any time.

In my opinion, no statistical evidence supports one strategy being superior to another. In the General Electric example, all the financial losses were the same. Had the trade been profitable, it would have shown you a greater reward in a more rapid fashion if you had taken the smallest risk per share, which equates to the greater share count. No style presented will provide you with a greater edge or a reduced risk.

The importance of the strategy is found within its ability to meet your realistic trading schedule. Adopting the correct strategy is of utmost importance. If you haven't thought about the strategy that is right for you, do so now.

# chapter 12

# Setting Stops

I have often heard that you know you are fluent in a language when you dream in that dialect. This makes a great deal of sense. After all, when something becomes so ingrained in your psyche, you no longer have to even think about that action; you just do it. This is true with both innate physical reactions, such as when my newborn child squints at a bright light or jumps at a loud noise, and with learned habits, such as buckling your seat belt when you enter an automobile. Many of our habitual learned activities are those that help us remain safe. This is no different from trading when it comes to setting stops. Just like when you buckle your seat belt or look both ways before crossing the street, stops must become so ingrained into your daily trading routine that they are nothing more than a natural part of your investing process. The litmus test of when you know you have truly embraced this idea is when your anxiety level doesn't increase from being in a trade, but instead increases only when you are in a trade without a stop.

When I first started trading stocks, I looked only for the opportunity for gain when I reviewed a stock, either long or short. I was so engrossed in the potential for profits that I never thought about the potential risk and, therefore, a stop was often an afterthought, if it was a thought at all. This thought process was flawed, and it hindered my growth. At present, when approaching any trade, a stop is the first thing I ponder, and it becomes the foundation from which my entire trading plan is developed. Whenever I review any potential trade, regardless of the direction, before going any further I first ask myself where a stop should be in the event I am wrong and the trade does not work.

A disciplined stop system is critical for proper execution and serves as the foundation for consistent success. While successful trading will ultimately be determined by profits, you will not be profitable on every trade taken. Therefore, to make money, your edge must give you a higher probability of profitable trades over losing trades throughout a longer period of time. In summary, your lasting success as a trader will be determined not by one individual trade, but by the continued execution of your overall trading strategy. It is for this reason that a losing trade may actually be considered successful if the trade was executed properly. As ridiculous as this sounds, it is imperative for you to understand this concept. The great stocks will flow into your account, as will many stinkers. The key is to keep all losses within the confines of your predetermined risk parameter so that you can continue exercising your edge regardless of losing trades. You can do this only by setting appropriate stop losses on each trade taken.

A fine line distinguishes remaining in control of a trade and basing your trade on mere hope. This line will always be quantified through your stop. Traders who experience consistent failure rather than consistent success often do so because they refuse to accept losses and move on. When a trade is no longer working, or the original idea you had for the trade is no longer valid, it becomes imperative for you to exit this position immediately. Changing your strategy or your ideas mid-trade is similar to a quarterback attempting to change the play after the ball has already been snapped. Sometimes such changes will work to your advantage, but more often than not they will result in a costly financial lesson. I often run into traders who refuse to adhere to proper discipline through stops, and because of their refusal they consistently cross the line from controlled trades into hope trades. Not only can the financial damage be significant, but spending days and nights hoping a trade starts to work in your favor is down-right exhausting. A trading journal, with a written trading plan for each stock, can help you remain accountable. However, only the self-discipline to adhere to your predetermined plan will foster success.

More than likely, you have experienced this world, where you are just watching and hoping a stock reverses to go in your favor so that you can either exit the trade for a smaller loss or possibly even a profit. Even if this reversal happens, the longer-term damage that occurs as a result is often worse than the loss that would have incurred if the stop were taken in the first place. Let me explain.

Imagine if you will, laying out a specific plan when approaching a stock. You have identified a pattern that may give you an edge and move in with your purchase or short sale with an identified area at which you would take the tradeoff if it did not work. Over a period of days, the stock reverses and quickly moves toward your predetermined stop. It is at this point that rather than preparing to exit, you begin to hope another reversal ensues. Soon, the trade falls below your stop, and rather than exit the trade, you decide to give it just a bit more time to see whether it will play out. You rationalize this behavior by accepting the small change as nonmaterial. Little do you realize this can be a very damaging decision with implications beyond the obvious financial loss. For this example, let's assume that instead of continuing its plummet, the trade reverses and not only returns to your basis but also shows you a profit. Instead of feeling proud of your execution, you feel relieved and empowered by your resiliency and fortitude, almost believing you were in a fight with the stock and came out ahead. Much like a criminal getting away with his first few crimes, you now have an ingrained belief that as long as you remain steadfast, you will ultimately be rewarded for your resiliency. Unfortunately, this bad habit will eventually catch up with you. Although it might not be the next trade or the trade thereafter, at some point a trade that goes beyond your original stop won't come back, but will instead inflict significant financial damage and erode your confidence level exponentially.

The key for you to realize is that all hope trades should be avoided. Whenever you feel you have crossed the line from being in control, to relying on hope, exit the trade immediately. Stops typically act as this line, and it is why respecting them can mean the difference between your sustained success and an eventual blow up.

Throughout the course of my trading career, I have come across a variety of stop strategies. I have also traded alongside those who set no stops at all. While I do believe that just adhering to any stop strategy is better than none at all, I also believe that most of the common strategies taught today only set up the trader for a tremendous amount of frustration. The strategy of stops is a subject that is neither dissected nor discussed nearly enough.

The most common stop strategy taught is based on a set percentage loss from which a stop can be placed. For example, I have often seen traders advocating a 5% or 10% stop loss on a trade. Of course, this can also be equated to a fixed dollar amount per share (for example, a stop of $.50 or $1 per share). As I stated, although

I do believe any stop strategy is better than none at all, I find significant flaws with a strategy that uses a fixed variable to determine the point at which one is incorrect.

Rather than a fixed variable across a variety of different trades I much prefer to set a stop based on a level at which the pattern that originally attracted me to the trade is no longer valid. To me, this makes much more sense and does not open one up to the susceptibility of being stopped out within a pattern that is still valid. Of course, this moves the discussion toward position sizing and risk management, a topic we cover in the next chapter.

Let's review again the Ford trade we used in a previous chapter (see Figure 12.1). Let's also assume that you have taken the trade in anticipation of a breakout, entering Ford at $7.50. Adhering to a fixed stop loss strategy, you subsequently set a stop loss order 5% below your initial entry point. While Ford did not dip at all in our previous example, imagine for a moment that the stock had dipped to $7.10, or a few pennies below the 5% limit from which you set your stop. I have indicated on the chart where you would have been stopped out. What is important to note is that Ford would not have broken down; instead, the stock would have continued moving within the pattern that attracted you in the first place. The question must therefore be asked: Was this a good stop? From an execution standpoint, I believe that laying out a plan and following it is what ultimately determines success and, therefore, the trade was successful. The question becomes this: Is there a better way to set a stop? Although it would be frustrating to be down 5% in unrealized losses, it would be even more frustrating if you were to stop out of Ford only to see the pattern work as was originally intended.

**Figure 12.1** *Ford breaking above the descending angular trend.*
Chart courtesy of Worden—www.Worden.com.

After reviewing your trade journal and cross-referencing the price action in Ford after you were stopped, it would be simple to declare that you just needed to widen your stop. You might even go so far as to adopt a new rule where you do not set a 5% stop, but rather an 8% stop, or maybe even a 10% stop. Again, it is important to relay that simply setting and adhering to a stop is excellent discipline. But what if there is a better way?

A few times in my career, I have worked with a trader who faced the dilemma of continuously being stopped out of a trade, only to see the trade move in the direction he suspected days later. The urge to simply widen the stops sets in. However, with this urge comes the potential for larger losses. On analyzing the strategy, I have found that typically the trader is setting a fixed percentage stop, rather than one that is unique to the pattern being played. With a case-specific small adjustment, the trader often eliminates this whipsaw action and many times remains in a trade, seeing it through to success instead of being stopped out prior to the desired move happening.

Your success in trading will often correlate with the finer points of execution that you will develop over time and through your growing experience. Take golf, for example, where a professional knows not only the appropriate club to use at each distance but also how to alter the club selection or swing for other variables, such as weather or where the ball is lying, be it in the rough or in the fairway. Professionals have learned this through years of experience, an intimate knowledge of their swing, and a full awareness of the performance they're anticipating. Weekend warriors, on the other hand, may have only a vague idea of what clubs to use and when, knowing they hit a wedge approximately 100 yards or a solid 3-iron 190. While using the appropriate clubs at roughly the correct distances is better than putting with a 3 iron, or using a driver in the sand trap, there is a big difference between the general knowledge of the weekend warrior and the intimate knowledge of the professional. This difference between the two golfers is typically reflected in their score after each round.

Let's look at a specific example that happened to me during the time I was writing this book. Figure 12.2 displays the stock of CBS Corp, which I viewed on January 15 as a potential trend change, and watched the stock break through an ascending trend line that began in late August. On seeing this action, I shorted shares of CBS Corp at $13.10 as a reactionary trade, placing a stop at $14. I used the $14 level as the point at which I would no longer believe the trend break to be valid, thus covering the stock and exiting for a loss. The trade did not initially go in the direction I desired. Instead, it moved higher over the next few days, trading as high as $13.92, just three days after I entered the trade. At this point, had I set a fixed stop of 5%, I would have been stopped out as the stock moved against me by 6.25%. After the bounce higher, CBS Corp reversed lower and spent the next several days meandering around my entry price, neither breaking up nor breaking down. After much back and forth, finally on February 3 the stock once again made a surge up, moving as high as 13.85, or 5.7% above my initial short entry At this level, I would have again been stopped out using a fixed 5% stop level. However, because my stop was placed at $14, rather than being stopped, I remained in the trade. After a few days, the stock once again reversed lower, and eventually started showing me a positive return to take partial gains on February 5, when the stock reached a low of $12.42, or 5% below my initial entry point of $13.10. This is a perfect, real-life example of how a dynamic stop kept me in a winning trade, as opposed to a fixed stop knocking me out of the trade before it eventually worked. Placing stops is as artistic as finding the patterns that will give you your edge toward profit. However, just as you identify the opportunity, there must be a corresponding level at which the opportunity is proven a failure and the trade must be removed.

**Figure 12.2** *CBS Corp breaking below an angular ascending trend.*
Chart courtesy of Worden—www.Worden.com.

Reviewing the previous trade strategies, using lateral and angular trend lines as your guide, in addition to the different methodologies anticipatory or reactionary, you should be able to identify the level at which a stop order would be placed for each trade taken.

If you recall from the preceding chapter, the reactionary trader or delayed reactionary trader waits for the desired move to occur before initiating a position. For example, if a lateral or angular trend line has been identified with a trade strategy developed to enter the position on a corresponding break of the trend, a stop strategy is relatively easy. The same trend line that was used to determine the breakout level may also be used as a guide from which to exit the trade.

For the purpose of this example, I have drawn angular and lateral trend lines to discuss the stop point noted in Figure 12.3 .For each chart, let's assume you have identified that the trade would be taken on a trend change rather than on a trend continuation. It is this same line that may then be used as a stop level. At times, a break of trend that reverses may happen the same day, and this is why you might want to wait until the day is nearing a close, and thus ensure the break is holding, before initiating the position. This delayed reactionary style may help to avoid being whipsawed and stopped out the same day. The risk is that you might miss a significant move if the initial break transpires early in the day and continues to move aggressively all throughout the day. In my opinion, you should learn to gauge this based on the environment you are in. If you are continuously missing out on large moves by waiting until the day's end, clearly an adjustment needs to be made by removing your hesitation.

Lateral Trend Line                    Angular Trend Line

**Figure 12.3**  *Sample lateral and angular trend lines.*

For reactionary traders, the stop is clear and should not be argued with. Setting stops while using an anticipatory strategy is not as simple. Setting stops for anticipatory trades is a bit challenging because you are entering the stock before the trend line you are watching has come into play. Because of this, you must look elsewhere to determine whether your trade is no longer valid. Most of the time, you can do this by finding an alternative trend line on the opposite side of the level you are watching. It does not matter whether the trend line you use to determine your stop is the same type of trend line you are using to determine the trade in the first place. For example, if you are anticipating a lateral trend break, but see a corresponding ascending trend below, you could easily use a move below the ascending trend line as your stop point. However, at times it may be a similar trend line. For example, identifying a lateral trend line above and a lateral trend line below would result in two key levels from which you could determine both the success of the trade and the stop level.

The charts shown in Figure 12.4 and Figure 12.5 illustrate this stop strategy and how it relates to anticipatory trading.

Every trade is different, and, like snowflakes, no two chart patterns are exactly alike. Although putting risk management guidelines in place via stops is essential, it is just as important to correlate your stop strategy with the opportunity that has developed. Doing so ensures that you remain in the trade to at least experience the pattern coming to fruition or see it negated altogether.

**Figure 12.4** *General Electric consolidating above and below angular trend lines.*

Chart courtesy of Worden—www.Worden.com.

**Figure 12.5** *IBM consolidating above and below lateral trend lines.*

Chart courtesy of Worden—www.Worden.com.

# chapter 13

# How to Trade the Trader

It had already been over an hour, and I could tell the entire plane was getting anxious. We hadn't moved more than 5 feet as the rain came down and the thunder continued to pound. Barely any air squeaked out of the overhead nozzle, and a toddler two rows in front of me was starting a fit of rage. Over the loudspeaker, the pilot updated us that our status had not changed, that we were still awaiting word on when we would be able to take off. I had experienced an exhausting 24 hours leading up to this, and I was getting a little frustrated. I had been in this situation many times before and doubted I would make it home to see my family any time soon.

Charlotte was a nice city, but not one where I wanted to spend the night. With my trusty smart phone, I pulled up the local weather map and saw that there was no chance of our storm letting up any time soon. I peered out my window to see at least 20 other planes in a similar situation, with another 10 or 15 waiting in an orderly line behind them on the runway. I made an educated guess that in a matter of minutes we would be pulling back into the airport and be grounded for the evening. My travel experience told me that to secure a hotel room I could not wait and had to act immediately. If I was wrong, a canceled room reservation would be a small price to pay to hedge my gut feel.

Instead of feverishly dialing the phone to call various hotels, bringing attention to what I was doing while sitting in my comfy aisle seat, I loaded up my phone's web browser, navigated to my favorite travel site, and booked a room at the closest available hotel. No more than five minutes after I had submitted my information, the pilot returned to the loudspeaker notifying us of our new evening plans, grounded in Charlotte. Within seconds, cell phones everywhere were out and being dialed. I listened as frantic travelers attempted to book reservations for only a limited number of rooms available to only the quickest fingers. Other unsuspecting and notably novice travelers looked around to those on the phone as if they too should be doing something. However, most had no clue what was to come next. The follow-up announcement from the flight attendant informed everyone that it was best to proceed to customer service where they could be rebooked for a morning flight and discuss evening accommodations. Yeah, right.

As I suspected, the gate was chaos when I exited the plane. Passengers had questions about baggage, compensation, travel arrangements, and hotel accommodations for the overworked agents. I dodged the madness and went as quickly as possible to ground transportation to find the next available cab. On my way, I passed the customer service counter and saw a line no less than 300 yards long. As I exited the baggage claim area and caught the next cab, I couldn't help but notice the mad group of travelers congregating around the hotel phone bank clamoring for what was sure to be a steady stream of sold-out hotel rooms. As I told the cab driver my destination, I placed a call to central reservations to start rebooking my own return flight the next morning. Thirty minutes later, after being checked in and now comfortable in my room, I thought about all that had just happened and couldn't help but recognize the similarities with this experience and trading.

For many years, the vast majority of traders had absolutely no clue about how best to approach the market. Considering that the market went on a 20-year bull run from 1980 to 2000, why should they? Numerous books were written and studies conducted concluding that all an investor needed to do was adhere to a balanced portfolio with a diversified mix of stocks and bonds. When the tech bubble of 2000 popped, the game changed. Slowly, a large group of investors began educating themselves about market movement, many of whom found a home within the world of technical analysis. Although the technology bubble was fierce, it didn't truly have a lasting effect because only a few short years after the market hit bottom it advanced to new all-time highs. Passive investors were rewarded for their patience, and once again most investors were lulled into a false sense of security. As time progressed, the arguments surrounding passive investing and diversification again took center stage.

But then there was 2008, the real game changer. The precipitous decline caught almost all passive investors and novice traders off guard, resulting in significant damage to their portfolios. A real bear market not seen since the early 1970s sparked a new wave of trading education when a vast majority of investors became fed up with traditional methods that clearly neither worked nor protected them from losses.

Most technical analysis traders did just fine in 2008, and I believe it is why this style immediately became popular among the investor crowd seeking a new way to manage their money. When significant multiyear uptrends were broken in the indices, those adhering to basic technical analysis principals didn't ask questions, they sold. Rather than hold onto hope that things would turn out okay, technical analysis traders acted on what they knew, protecting themselves from one of the most vicious declines in history. This did not go unnoticed and almost overnight, a flood of new traders studying everything from moving averages to stochastics emerged on the scene.

Rooted in its ability to take advantage of a crowd's emotional behavior, this seismic shift of the crowd itself has challenged the basic principals from which technical analysis was developed in the first place. With its newfound popularity, you can no longer adhere to only the basic technical analysis principals with the utmost confidence they will work. Like sitting on the plane, you must think one step ahead of the other traders and consider their moves before they make them. The true edge must now be found in trading these traders who are trading these patterns.

Now that you have a basic understanding of pattern recognition, along with a proper stop methodology, you need to know how to proceed with a trade-the-trader strategy. An effective phrase used often in trading says *from failed moves come fast moves*. The concept is simple. When so many are looking for the same move to occur, if this move does not transpire all those traders will be like the airline passengers heading for the exits simultaneously. This creates an incredible opportunity because so many traders must now reverse their positions, thus sparking a significant move that you can capitalize on.

The challenge with this strategy is knowing when to use it and when to refrain. Suppose, for example, that your previous two breakout trades resulted in a loss. It could be easy for you to conclude that these trades were anomalies and the next trade would be a success. However, quite possibly there may be a different issue in play. What if the strategy is no longer to buy breakouts but to short their failure? Meaning that, rather than buy a stock which has moved above a lateral trend line resistance point, the profitable play is to wait for this move to fail, at which point you would short the stock, seeking to capitalize on its decline.

Let's assume for a moment that rather than take the next breakout trade you wait to see whether it follows the similar pattern of your previous two. When the trade punctures the level you were watching, it does in fact reverse, and rather than be thankful you did not enter this trade, you short the reversal with a stop over the high prior to the reversal. Odds are that what just happened is you capitalized on the misfortune of others who attempted to buy the breakout and were subsequently stopped out.

Let's discuss a simple example assuming a stock had been trending higher and was approaching a key resistance level around $50. The stock looked and acted healthy, and it was obvious a break above the lateral trend line at $50 would lead to much higher prices. After some consolidating, the stock does in fact break above $50. Shortly after it does, however, it reverses quickly and closes the day below the $50 breakout level. In a traditional technical analysis strategy, you may have bought this break out, subsequently being stopped out once the reversal set in. Consider the fact that you were not the only one who saw this pattern, nor were you the only one who acted on this pattern. The number of traders following this strategy could be significant, thus creating an incredible amount of force once the traditional stop on the failure was taken. However, rather than entering the stock long on the breakout, let's assume you would move in with a short position, seeking to capitalize on the downward thrust once the breakout failed. Odds favor a significant thrust lower, considering the vast amount of traders needing to reverse their positions once they realize traditional technical analysis did not work. The strategy you would have just used combined traditional technical analysis with the understanding of what the masses were doing and capitalizing on their movement. Once the traditional pattern failed, you made your move with a much higher probability of reward.

I have gained experience trading the trader in a variety of ways. I have gone long patterns that were traditional short setups, and shorted patterns that were traditional long setups. I have done this only after I have seen with my own eyes these basic technical-analysis patterns fail in other stocks I was observing at the time. My trading is now evolving to become much more based on trading traditional pattern failures than it is on trading the traditional patterns themselves.

Figure 13.1 shows a daily chart of Halliburton from October 2009. I have drawn a key lateral trend line I identified and also noted on the chart what is traditionally a head and shoulders topping pattern. Basic technical analysis tells us that the best way to capitalize on this pattern is to look for the lateral trend line connecting the shoulders to act as resistance, thus moving in with a short on the stock in that area. While on the surface Halliburton looked as if it was rolling over, displaying all the attributes of a traditional technical analysis top, I had noticed peculiar strength in other oil and gas stocks in April 2010 and was curious if Halliburton would follow suit. If the head and shoulders pattern failed, my profits would come from going long Halliburton once the traditional short area was surpassed and those who had been betting against Halliburton were forced to cover. Rather than

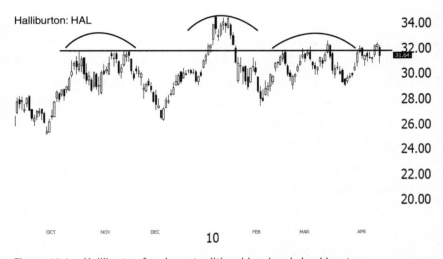

**Figure 13.1** *Halliburton forming a traditional head and shoulders top.*

Chart courtesy of Worden—www.Worden.com.

**Figure 13.2** *Halliburton moving higher after a failed head and shoulders top.*

Chart courtesy of Worden—www.Worden.com.

anticipate pattern failure, I wanted to see this lateral trend line surpassed before I entered the trade. I waited patiently for the break
up to occur. On April 20, the break did in fact take place, and I
entered a long side trade above $32. Once the stock breached this
level, as noted in Figure 13.2, it shot up quickly, confirming my
suspicion that a large group of traders were forced to cover their
shorts. The trade became quite profitable in just a few short days.

Trading pattern failures can be a dangerous game. I do not recommend those who only trade in an anticipatory manner to
embark on such a strategy, because you will only be guessing that
a specific pattern will not work. It has been my experience that
trading pattern failures is best done only after the traditional pattern has in fact failed, thereby giving you a clear level from which
to place your stop.

**Figure 13.3** *IBM breaking a traditional descending angular trend.*
Chart courtesy of Worden—www.Worden.com.

Figure 13.3 shows a daily chart of IBM on which I have drawn
a descending angular trend from the top in January. On April 14,
the stock broke above this descending trend and proceeded to follow through with close to a $3 move. However, five trading days

IBM: IBM

132.00
130.00
128.00
126.00
Failed Break   124.00

DEC        10        FEB        MAR        APR

**Figure 13.4**   *IBM falling back below the descending angular trend.*

Chart courtesy of Worden—www.Worden.com.

later, as noted in Figure 13.4, IBM abruptly fell back below the descending angular trend, resulting in a failed break. Had you taken this stock long, you would have been stopped out on a move back below the breakout level, resulting in a losing trade. Had you passed on the long rather waiting for a failure to occur, you could have had a significant profit once the stock begun its decline just a few days later. Although I didn't short this pattern at that time, it was one of the many clues that gave me trepidation over the market as a whole in April 2010, allowing me not only to avoid the subsequent decline but profit in other areas.

Trading these patterns is no different from trading basic pattern recognition. You at first identify your target and wait patiently for the opportunity to develop. When it does, you simply move in, setting your desired stop at the point where the pattern would no longer be valid. Because pattern failure typically comes from a reversal trapping those traders playing a basic technical analysis strategy, it makes sense to use a stop at the level that would correspond to the reversal point. In the IBM example, the high on April

19 was 132.28, making this level a logical point at which to place a stop, had you shorted the stock once the failure took place.

I believe that 2009 was a year filled with pattern failure. Most of the time, it was bearish patterns turned bullish that caught unsuspecting shorts off guard and resulted in incredible snaps higher. It was through this that I first began exploring the impact of the number of traders looking to play basic pattern recognition. My findings have altered my strategy ever since.

I do not believe basic pattern recognition should be avoided altogether. There will still be many instances where patterns you see emerging will in fact play out in the manner they traditionally should. You do, however, need to adhere to a level of flexibility that gives you the courage to step in should these patterns reverse and move in the opposite direction. This cannot be based on what you think will transpire or what you feel should occur. This can only be rooted in your observations and pursued through the same trading strategy as you would with any other opportunity.

What separated me from the masses in the Charlotte airport was nothing more than experience. I knew how the crowd would react, and I knew the only way to ensure my overnight sanity was to move one step ahead of the crowd's actions. I am sure others did the same, and they were the ones occupying the other rooms. I was not alone in my thinking, but I was in a much smaller group and therefore able to take advantage of the situation rather than be directed by it. Trading is no different, and the more that flock to basic technical analysis, the more important it will be to be moving one step ahead of the crowd seeking to profit from the failure of these patterns.

As you pursue your trading path, it is imperative you first become familiar with basic pattern recognition. Only through this solid understanding of the basics will you have the confidence and ability to explore other opportunities. Do not become overwhelmed by the thought of trading the trader, but do understand that you are not alone in your pursuit. To truly succeed, you must elevate your game above others and seek to capitalize on where their education ends.

# chapter 14

# Using and Controlling Risk to Your Advantage

"How much are you willing to lose on this trade?"

*Risk* is a buzzword within the financial world that can lead to a multitude of conversations. Commonly, your risk tolerance is how much stock exposure you should have at all times. This is an interpretation laughed at by every successful trader I know. The idea that you should always have stock exposure and the level should equate with your age or time horizon assumes that you have no ability to know when to move in or out of the market. I would take this a step further to say that adopting this definition of risk assumes that market timing isn't even possible. If that is the case, I guess it is just a matter of time before the hundreds of successful traders I know, making consistent gains day in and day out to feed their families, go belly up. Sorry to all of my trading friends out there; it's been fun.

The other common theme related to risk is its relationship with reward. We've all heard the general idea that if you take a greater risk, you have the potential for a greater reward. When it comes to trading stocks, I think this is the biggest crock going. If you believe this even remotely, I encourage you to purge this from your brain when approaching a successful trading strategy that seeks to make consistent profits over time. The "more reward for more risk" thesis insinuates that for you to make money trading you have to constantly put yourself in a position of potentially great loss. In reality, nothing is further from the truth. Successful trading is about quantifying and controlling your risk from the beginning to the end of each and every trade you take. It is this understanding of risk that will separate you in terms of longevity within the trading world.

I come across many traders who, despite their best efforts, cannot remove the gambling philosophy from their trading. Maybe this relates to you. Are you occasionally enticed to buy a stock you see plummeting? Or perhaps you're tempted to short a stock you believe simply cannot go any higher? How about taking a chance on an earnings report or an FDA announcement within the biotech world? The allure of rapid riches entices many. However, absolutely nothing good can come from acting on these temptations. Although financial calamity is possible, the biggest danger in venturing away from your disciplined trading strategy is actually the potential for success in the trade.

Suppose, for instance, that you witness a stock falling sharply to depths you never thought possible. So, you ask yourself, "What's the harm in taking a few shares at these levels?" With no set strategy, rather more like a crap shot, you take a few shares. Your timing couldn't have been better, and within moments the stock reverses and your gamble pays off. You might believe this is the mark of a great trader when actually it is the start of your gradual demise. Not only does the money flow in from the trade, but others congratulate you as if you had some innate knowledge of what would happen. The combination of an increased financial position and superficial confidence is deadly. The next time an opportunity develops that is similar, odds favor you taking the trade again with greater confidence because of the result of the previous bet. It is only a matter of time until the tables turn and the outcome is not favorable at all. You must avoid these major financial and emotional setbacks. The only way to do so is to disregard the notion that says the greater reward comes from the greatest risk. Sustained reward in trading does not come from taking exorbitant risk but in calculating your acceptable risk and utilizing your edge over a large enough sample set of trades.

In short, the two basic principals about risk as discussed in the mainstream are a far cry from how they are discussed in successful trading circles. Furthermore, successful traders have, for the most part, given up on trying to convince the masses of this and have come to the conclusion that time and again most investors will just be led blindly to slaughter by those attempting to educate them about traditional and unrealistic ideas of risk.

If I were to ask you what you would be willing to lose before taking a trade, what would your answer be? Maybe you would chuckle and say zero. While humorous, this is already poor execution, setting you up for consistent frustration and ultimate failure. Whenever you approach any trade, the first variable you must understand and embrace is the amount of money you are willing to lose on the trade. Just as you would write down the reasoning behind the trade—the pattern you have recognized, and where you would be wrong (i.e., your stop)—you should note the amount of money you are willing to lose on the trade if you see the trade through from start to finish. Risk is as simple as that and can be defined as the amount of money you are willing to lose to see whether your pattern-recognition read plays out as you believe it could.

Earlier I discussed a plan that had me entering a plethora of trades. My goal was simple. I wanted to take my proven edge and increase my sample set in the same way a casino expands its gaming floor, thus increasing my rate of return. This did not pan out as I hoped. The end result had me exhausted and frustrated. Rather than increase my profits by increasing my sample set, I learned to increase my returns by gradually increasing the amount I risk on each trade. I find myself trading less while seeking out only the best opportunities, instead of taking them all. It is peaceful, profitable, and most important, scalable.

As a trader, before entering any trade, you should set a fixed dollar amount or portfolio percentage you are willing to lose. For example, I manage a public portfolio tied to a subscription service whereby I send email alerts for every trade I execute. When I launched the portfolio, I allocated $100,000 to begin the account. Within this portfolio, my risk per trade is .5% of the portfolio, or $500. The hedge fund I manage is much larger, and the dollar amounts are significantly increased. Because I'm managing a much larger pool of money here, I am susceptible to liquidity issues and am not as flexible. I have learned that a typical risk of .2% of the portfolio is acceptable for each trade. Finally, my most passive management service, separately managed accounts, possess a much longer time frame, seeking to capitalize on patterns that may take weeks to months to play out. I have found that a risk between .5% and 1% per trade is acceptable.

I encourage you to find an amount based on your trading capital somewhere between .2% and .5%. Regardless of the amount, the importance lies in you knowing exactly what the amount is you are willing to lose before you ever place a trade. Not only is this psychologically important, but as you will soon see, it is the first variable from which we will build our entire trading strategy.

So, what is your risk value? Determining this value might prove a bit tricky. In my opinion, while you are learning and honing your skills, your risk level must be something that is extremely palatable. The key when you are learning and refining your strategy is not to let the risk dictate your trades. Instead, you want to become comfortable embracing the risk on each trade. You must be able to execute your trades without any outside influence, such as worrying about the potential for loss. The risk does not determine the trade, you determine your risk.

I often hear people discussing paper trading as a way to learn trading. While, in theory, learning to trade without having any financial risk makes a great deal of sense, it will not help you. Regardless of what the risk per trade is, an immediate emotional connection attaches to the trade when real money is on the line. Rather than paper trading, when you are learning, I believe it important to just use an extremely low risk per trade, but to at least be financially committed to some degree. At almost all levels, commissions become a factor. However, when you start down this road, do not let the brokerage commissions influence your decision making. Consider these an educational cost; after all, your future benefit will be far greater when you eventually increase your risk per trade.

You might not be in a position to pursue your trading plan with real capital, in which case you are currently at a disadvantage. If there is no other option but to paper trade, you must have a set plan in place, as if it were your actual money. There can be no trades where you believe "such and such will happen" and therefore take 1,000 paper shares on a whim. It is imperative that you practice as if you were trading real money, quantifying your risk per trade, setting your stops, and executing the trade strategy we'll continue to discuss. Paper trading will never replace the true emotions of having real money on the line, but done properly it will at least allow you to follow a specific strategy and learn the methods you will utilize to become successful.

Take a moment now to ponder what you would be willing to risk on each trade. When in doubt, start with a value that is lower. You can always increase this, and in fact will do so as your confidence and skill set improve. In addition to your risk per trade, spend some time thinking about your total acceptable portfolio risk, assuming you have more than one trade going at any given time. It is not enough to mentally accept the individual trade risk, but you also must accept the total potential loss should you be stopped out of every position you are in. Predetermining this amount will allow you to set a limit to the number of stocks you will hold at the same time.

For those new to this strategy, I recommend starting at .2% with no more than four positions on at a time. If you are trading with $50,000, your risk per trade is $100, with a total of $400 at risk, if you are in fact in all four trades. This should allow you to proceed with trades without an overwhelming fear of great potential losses. If this amount creates anxiety, it is too high and you should reduce it even further. Over time, you should increase this in increments of .1% until you get to a level that is sustainable and sufficient, such as .5%.

It might be easy to sit back and ponder a specific risk value or percentage, but understand that this is an evolving exercise and one that must be continuously reviewed as you grow as a trader. Your ongoing success as a trader will correlate quite a bit with how honest you are with yourself and your inner feelings. It isn't enough to simply set a risk value, if you don't truly own that risk value. Owning the risk value means that after the trade is placed, you have emotionally and psychologically accepted the fact that you may very well lose the risk value you have established. Once the trade is placed, if the potential for loss makes you uncomfortable at all, it is an indication that your risk value is too high. If this emotion comes into play, it will soon influence your decision making, and will hinder your growth both emotionally and financially as a trader. It is of extreme importance to establish a specific risk value, implement it, and own it throughout each and every trade. Furthermore, it is important to set a risk value that can be adhered to for a large enough sample set, in my opinion at least 20 trades, without the trader feeling the need to immediately reduce the risk because of a string of losses.

After you have determined your appropriate risk level per trade, and your acceptable total portfolio risk, remain consistent with these risk levels. You may fall into the trap of increasing risk because a specific trade appeals to you more than another. Whenever you increase or decrease your risk levels, it is imperative to remain consistent for at least the next ten trades. Increasing risk on one trade, which may result in a loss, then subsequently reducing risk once this loss occurs, will only increase the number of profitable trades needed to make up the previous loss. An ever-changing risk value will lead to an erratic and ever-changing equity curve for your portfolio. Identify your appropriate risk levels and stick with them.

# Controlling Risk

One of the most potentially damaging aspects of trading is when a position or portfolio takes a drawdown that is outside the bounds of a normal drop. This amount may vary for different traders. However, any portfolio draw in excess of 20% will typically inflict emotional and financial wounds that may damage a trader's confidence to the point of no return. Successful traders rarely if ever allow this to happen, not because they select better stocks or because they have a better handle on market movement, but because they manage risk and understand this is paramount to their ongoing success. At any given time, you should know precisely how much risk you have exposed yourself to and be comfortable with that amount. It is not uncommon for me to review my portfolio risk several times a day, either adjusting stops or cutting share counts, to make sure this risk remains acceptable. Unless you are all cash, it is impossible to eliminate your risk altogether. However, it is quite possible to remain in control of your risk at all times.

Understanding your initial risk value per trade is essential. However, you cannot stop there. You also need to understand what I call your initial and live portfolio risk. This is the total value of losses you would experience if every position you had is stopped out simultaneously. Although it is rare that this would happen, it is helpful to know what you have exposed yourself to, in the event it does. It is this calculation that is essential for you to know at any given point during any given day. I believe that knowing this value has allowed me to continuously achieve new account highs despite minor setbacks through my normal and acceptable portfolio drawdowns.

To calculate this, I commissioned the development of a program called the Risk Analyzer that evolved from a basic spreadsheet. On this spreadsheet, I manually update my current positions, including their current stop loss values and their current prices. Multiplying my share count for each times the difference between the current stock price and stop price gives me my live risk per trade. I then total this live risk per trade to give me my total live portfolio risk. Thankfully, I no longer have to manually input all this data because the program I developed, calculates this information for me. In many instances, I have cut positions or eliminated them altogether if I felt my live portfolio risk was too high. I have outlined a brief example of what this would look like for a mixed portfolio of three stocks, each taken with an approximate risk of $500 (see Table 14.1). In this example, you can assume that each trade has been taken and is still trading within the price from which the trade was executed, thereby showing the initial per trade risk.

Table 14.1   *Total Portfolio Risk*

| Stock | Long/Short | Current Price | Stop | Risk per Share | Shares | Total Risk |
|-------|-----------|---------------|------|----------------|--------|------------|
| XYZ | Short | 35.16 | 36.50 | 1.34 | 373 | $500 |
| XYZ | Short | 12.95 | 14.00 | 1.05 | 475 | $500 |
| XYZ | Long | 22.50 | 20.05 | 2.45 | 204 | $500 |
| | | | | | | $1,500 |

Although this is a good start, the markets are continuously in motion. Therefore, your live risk is continuously in flux. To maintain a true understanding of your live risk, the current price column must be updated to reflect the changes in stock movement.

It is not enough to mentally own the initial stock risk, but you must also mentally own the live portfolio risk. In the past, I used to call the unrealized gains in my account *house money*. I would say things like "playing with houses money" and "the trade is now risk free." This mindset was not only wrong, but also very dangerous, in that when a reversal set in I was constantly not only giving back the houses money but also taking a draw through the initial risk. In hindsight, I was far too cavalier when I was in trades that were going in my favor. I needed to look at the unrealized gains not as house money but as my money and to count these gains as risk, just as I would the initial risk I had taken on the trade. When I finally embraced this, it changed my trading forever and dramatically increased the speed at which my equity curve rose.

You must understand, embrace, and accept your live portfolio risk when your stocks are moving and changing in price. When trades are going in your favor, your live portfolio risk grows exponentially and becomes much greater than the initial risk should the trade reverse and be stopped out. Most of the time, a trader will not calculate this risk for unrealized gains. However, I have found that unrealized gains are just as important to understand and embrace. A common pitfall when the market is moving in the direction of your trades is for you to add more positions without updating your live portfolio risk. Initially, these new trades may show you a greater profit. However, I have personally seen great damage done when the market reverses abruptly, not only stopping you out of new positions that never showed a profit but also taking away unrealized gains.

To review this change, let's assume for a moment that each trade on our previous example advanced in your desired direction

10% and for the time being no new positions were added (see Table 14.2).

Table 14.2    *Total Portfolio Risk*

| Stock | Long/Short | Current Price | Stop | Risk per Share | Shares | Total Risk |
|-------|-----------|---------------|------|----------------|--------|------------|
| XYZ | Short | 31.64 | 36.50 | 4.86 | 373 | $1,812.78 |
| XYZ | Short | 11.66 | 14.00 | 2.34 | 475 | $1,111.50 |
| XYZ | Long | 24.75 | 20.05 | 4.70 | 204 | $958.80 |
| | | | | | | $3,883.08 |

You may assume that the live portfolio risk would increase by the same 10% amount, when in reality it more than doubles from a total of $1,500 in our first table to $3,883.08 after the current prices of the stocks are updated. Yes, these are unrealized gains, but this calculation is now the real portfolio risk you face if you were to be stopped out of all positions after they have already moved in your favor 10%. While trades are in existence and moving, this calculation can help you can gain a much better understanding of what you stand to lose in real dollars if your stops are hit. If you cannot accept this live risk and do not feel comfortable with this exposure, either the position needs to be reduced or your stops need to be raised. The next chapter addresses this when we delve further into the trading strategy.

I hope, by now, you are looking at risk in a completely different way and realize just how important it is within a successful trading plan. I cannot stress enough how important it is to mentally own the risk from the perspective of each individual trade, but also from the perspective of the entire portfolio. Failure to mentally own this risk will allow emotions to control your trading, and you will fall into the trap of making erratic decisions in the heat of the moment. If you haven't done so already, think about what you are comfortable with as an acceptable risk per trade amount. Also ponder what you are willing to accept as a live portfolio risk at any given moment. Write these numbers down, keep them by your trading station, and firmly implant them into your brain. Do not view them as negatives but as allies and guardrails for you in your new journey of successful trading.

° The risk analyzer is available at www.tickerville.com.

# chapter 15

# Taking Gains

"So tell me, when do I sell?"

Do you expect gains or are you surprised by them? I'll never forget one of my first successful trades under the tutelage of Rev Shark. I had stalked a pattern for several days while the stock methodically set up to my liking. Although I don't recall the company, I can still see the bullish pennant in my mind as the chart wound tighter and tighter below its descending trend line and above its ascending trend line, creating a pennant (as the name suggests). The pattern projected the possibility that a rather large break was coming. Because I sat in front of my computer day in and day out, I did not feel the need to enter in anticipation of the break. Instead, I waited for the break to occur and resolved to react when it happened. Since I was reacting to a trend break, I made a mental note that if and when the break came, my stop would be a failure of the same break I was buying.

Finally, after days of observation I watched the stock start to break above the descending trend line I had drawn from the recent peak. Volume was high, and I didn't hesitate to pounce when the time was right. The stock broke out above the trend line and caught significant momentum. The gain for that day was larger than I had experienced in any short-term trade I had ever taken. To say I was excited was an understatement, and I wasn't shy in relaying my enthusiasm to my then trading mentor. I couldn't wait for the accolades I was sure to receive. I was certain he would pat me on the back and give me a quick high five, fanning my growing confidence flame. I'll never forget when he looked right at me and told me to sit down and relax. It was a harsh tone, as if I had done something wrong, and I felt a sense of shock and disbelief. I was angry that my excitement was just zapped with a few quick words. However, I was anxious to hear what he had to say next. Without missing a beat, Rev sternly looked my way and with as cold a face as I had ever seen said simply, "Expect gains; do not be surprised by them."

Those words have rung in my ears since. This one comment sparked the honest realization that I viewed trading as a gamble rather than a controlled vehicle for consistent profits. At the core, I believed successful trading had more to do with luck than skill. It was a harsh realization of just how much I needed to grow.

I am going to assume that you may possess the same mindset as I did, and not truly expect gains. When gains come, you are as surprised by them as I was, and if you are honest with yourself you might admit that accepting losses is actually easier than accepting gains, simply because it is much more familiar.

The goal of what you are learning here is first and foremost to develop a solid strategy, giving you a defined edge from which to consistently profit. However, it is just as important to remove those profits from the market so that your equity curve is steadily on the rise. What good is it to trade successfully and not withdraw those profits from the market to build your own account?

If there is one area of trading that is rarely, if ever, discussed, it is the strategy of taking profits. I find it interesting that hundreds of books are written on how to trade stocks, which subsequently attract millions of readers seeking to do just that, with little or no discussion about what to do next. It seems to me more traders are interested in finding the next great stock than they are in producing incremental and consistent gains.

You may also make the assumption that once a profit occurs you know what to do when your strategy actually works. I can personally attest to the fact that even when I finally had a firm grasp on pattern recognition and a solid understanding of when and where to enter trades, I still knew nothing about appropriate trade management and how to realize my gains. It was if I had acquired all the variables needed to make money but had no strategy whatsoever on how to keep it. This lack of understanding resulted in a very chaotic and erratic equity curve. I would go on large runs, as profits seemed to flow easily into my account, but would then experience incredible drawdowns taking me back to where I started or even below. I had learned to make money and expect gains, but my actual equity growth was far from consistent and always relied on my general feel for when to get out of my positions and raise cash.

At times, this feel worked just fine for me. However, when I annually reviewed my trading sheets and journals, I realized that I was often selling far too early, or at times, far too late. Although my general feel was better than that of most investors, it was far from consistent. What I needed was a system for managing my trades that removed my "feel" from the equation altogether. At the urging of a dear trading friend, I adopted a systematic way to take gains that built on my existing strategy of individual trade risk. I decided to start taking profits at levels that were a multiple of my initial risk per trade. This system was yet another piece of the puzzle to round out a solid trading strategy that now produces consistent returns, regardless of the market direction.

My profit-taking system is rather simple, in that gains are taken at one and two times my initial risk level for the trade. At each level, I sell or cover a third of my initial position. Unlike when I set stops, these profit targets are based solely on multiples of risk and are not a technical view of where a particular stock could go. While I have experimented with many profit-taking strategies, the calculated method described is unemotional and consistent. Once a profit target is realized, I adjust my stop on remaining shares to ensure my now profitable trade does not turn into a losing trade. When the stock moves past twice my initial risk level, thereby leaving me with one-third of my original share count, I keep the remaining shares with the possibility of a larger move evolving over time. While my profit-taking system is not designed to hold large positions through substantial moves, it is effective in booking continuous profits within successful trades. Although you will never hit the proverbial homerun, the multitude of singles and doubles will result in what should become a continuously rising equity curve.

Let's look at an example. Your trade-management system, if you use my approach, begins first and foremost with your individual risk per trade. For the purpose of this example, let's assume that you are adhering to a $300 risk per trade. You are considering a long position in stock XYZ, which is selling for $12 per share. You note that the trade would no longer be valid if the stock drops to $11 per share. So you place your stop at this level. Taking the difference between the entry price and your stop price, you calculate that you can buy 300 shares, risking $1 per share and, thus, your $300 risk limit. Shortly after you enter the trade, the stock begins to rise and in a matter of a few days achieves your first profit target of $13 or your initial risk ($1) added to your initial purchase price ($12). It is at this point where you sell one-third of your shares, or 100 shares, locking in an initial profit of $100, less transaction costs. After selling one-third of your position, you then raise your stop from the original $11 per share to your entry point of $12 per share, ensuring you do not allow a winning trade to turn into a losing trade. In this particular example, we'll assume your stock continues to rise and in a matter of days trades at your second profit target of $14, or twice your original risk. As with your first sale, you again sell another 100 shares, or one-third of your position at your second profit level, locking in another $200, less transaction costs. At this time, you raise your stop from your previously raised $12 to your first profit target of $13. In the event the trade reverses at this point and stops you out, you at least secure another $100 on your final 100 shares, again not allowing your trade to turn from a winner into a loser. Now that you have achieved your second profit level, it is at this point where the trade-management strategy allows for the final one-third position to move freely. Should the stock continue to advance, you will participate in the move with your final 100 shares. In the event the advance comes to an end, resulting in a reversal and a decline, your final 100 shares should stop out at your second profit target of $14, resulting in another $200 gain.

You can customize your profit strategy however you like, and there may be a multitude of methods from which you can pursue a similar strategy. I strongly encourage all strategies to include two basic principals: booking partial gains as the stock is becoming profitable and raising stops to ensure profits do not become losses.

You may have already started to wonder why I don't recommend pyramiding into a position, whereby you actually add more exposure when the trade is working. Or why I don't recommend the general rule that you should let winners run and cut your losers quickly. Interestingly enough, I have explored and utilized both strategies and found that personal emotions became too big a factor when it came to trade management. What this meant was that my emotions were controlling my trading, which could be influenced by a wide range of variables, including anything from my general feel of the market to how I was physically feeling that day. With no set strategy, I had no guidelines to follow to help me to know when to sell and take gains.

At first, I resisted the thought of a system that booked gains as soon as a stock showed a profit. This negative feeling was trumped by my desire to maintain an increasingly rising equity curve. After using this trade-management system for several years now, it will remain with me forever. There is something invigorating about seeing a continuous flow of profits into my account. Even when stops are taken on winning trades, they are done so in correlation with profits and so as not to let winners turn into losers.

The system works for short positions in the same manner as longs, such as our previous example. Let's review a trade I had while writing this book (see Figure 15.1). In January 2010, I had been drawn to a potential short in Albemarle because the stock had been flirting with a breakdown of an angular ascending trend going back to early March. My first attempt to short Albemarle was on January 27, and was stopped out just a few days later. I continued to watch the name for a potential setup to transpire from which I could reenter the short. I got my chance on February 4, when the stock once again pushed through the trend line looking as though it would have some follow through to the downside.

**Figure 15.1** *Albemarle Corp breaking below an ascending angular trend.*
Chart courtesy of Worden—www.Worden.com.

Although I actually took this trade within my fund, for the purpose of this example I'll use a different risk calculation, using the same price per share that was actually executed: assuming my risk was $1,000 for the trade, and entering the short trade at $35.91 with a stop over the day high of $36.50. As a side note, I chose my stop over the day high because I felt that if this stock were to reverse over this level I would no longer want to be in the trade because the move would negate the trend break. The difference between my entry point of $35.91 and my stop $36.50 was .59. This meant I was able to sell short 3,389 shares to keep my risk for the trade at my $1,000 limit. I immediately calculated my first profit level so that I could place a limit order to cover one-third of my shares at this level in the event I was away from my desk or the stock moved too quickly for me to actually enter the order.

With a risk of .59 per share, this put my first profit target at $35.32. I achieved this level the next day as the stock continued its decline. At this level, I covered one-third of my position, or 1,130 shares, locking in a profit of $667 dollars. Immediately, I lowered the stop on my remaining shares to my entry price of $35.91. I also set a new limit order to cover another one-third of the shares at my second profit target of $34.73. It just so happened that on this particular day the sell-off was rather vicious, and I achieved my second profit target just a few hours later. I covered another 1,130 shares, locking in an additional profit of $1,333.40. My realized gain thus far on the trade was slightly over $2,000. Once my second profit target was achieved, I raised the stop on my remaining one-third to my first profit target of $35.32 and let the final shares move accordingly.

When using a risk-multiple profit-taking strategy, you might review a pattern you find favorable and note how the technical action may be suggesting the stock's next move. In such a case, your first concern is to consider the point at which you would be wrong, thereby determining your stop. You should also consider the general potential for profit based on the risk multiple. As a general rule of thumb, I do not advise entering into a trade that does not look as if three times your initial risk is possible. Although you might not know this for certain, you can gain a general feel just by reviewing congestion areas that fall above or below the point at which you would be taking the trade.

For example, suppose you find a stock worthy of shorting. The stock has been consolidating in a fairly narrow range, indicating a breakdown may be forthcoming. The stock is trading at $25 per share, and you note that a breakdown level would be approximately $24.50. In addition to the breakdown level, you note that a reversal back up to $26 would negate the trade, and thus give you a total risk per share of $1.50 if the trade triggered ($26 – $24.50). As you review the pattern, you note that several months ago the stock was trading lower and spent a considerable amount of time around $20. Based on your read of the chart, it is clear that this level would provide a significant amount of support. While not guaranteed, you assume that if the stock were to break your level of $24.50, the stock would at least pause around $20. Because your risk per share is $1.50, three times this risk would be $4.50. Because your trade would trigger at $24.50, achieving a multiple of three times your risk would place the stock at $20, the area in which you see significant support. From your vantage point, this trade is presenting you with at least three times your initial risk and is worthy of your capital.

Let's assume that rather than $20 you noted that the longer-term support was at $22. As a logical area for where the stock may stop declining, this presents you with a potential reward of slightly below two times your initial risk. This would no longer be as favorable a risk profile as the previous example and is not worthy of your trading dollars. As you become more familiar with chart patterns and logical areas of support and resistance, calculating the approximate risk profile for a given trade will become easier. There was a time in my trading when I would swing for the proverbial fences, seeking outsized returns by taking outsized risk. The results were erratic and at times yielded great returns, but rarely allowed for sustained progress. Regardless of how great the success, it seemed I always went through extreme periods of heavy drawdowns. This emotional roller coaster led me to develop a trading system that seeks much more consistent and sustainable returns. Over time, this resulted in a steadily rising equity curve, correlating with a much more balanced and unemotional approach to trading.

No matter how long you trade or how successful you become, you will still face challenges. I now find myself struggling to keep my final third piece after my trade has already reached my first and second profit targets. The allure of booking the entire gain becomes too great, and I find myself closing out the position time and again. It is a good problem to have, but one that I am personally trying to improve. No matter how successful you become, you can always find areas to improve on. This is one of the exciting challenges presented through the world of trading stocks. Embrace this challenge and meet each obstacle head on. Not only will you improve as a result, your equity curve will also nicely reflect this progression.

# chapter 16

# Reviewing the Entire Plan

Let's take a look at the trading strategy we have laid out so far.

## Chart Work

The strategy begins with the arduous process of navigating through a multitude of charts. I encourage you to make this a daily routine. If your schedule does not allow you to sift through charts on a daily basis, find a consistent time that works for you. This is the foundation to build on. If you skip this step, you might as well make a check payable to Mr. Market and call it a day. I have a rule that I live by: No chart work, no trading. It is through this process that you gain a feel for the underlying stock action within the market. You should not rely on the opinion of others. More often than not, they are guessing anyway. In fact, the more chart work you do on your own, the more you will view outside opinions as nothing more than noise. It is why the greats worked in silence, and it is why my staff, who sit in offices just around the corner from me, communicate with me through instant messaging. I realize it's a bit manic, but it works. Your routine may consist of going through all charts within the NASDAQ 100, the S&P 500, or a variation of the two. Through this continuous process, you will become familiar with the underlying charts and their daily movement. Over time, you will begin to feel the rhythm of the market. Through this tedious but rewarding process, you will seek out patterns that will become your trading opportunities. It is imperative to let these patterns come to you. More than likely, you will initially see certain patterns that may or may not exist. In due time, this will subside. As you see how stocks develop firsthand, you will observe how the patterns resolve themselves. I encourage you to review the same stocks (and not new ones each time) again and again so that you become familiar with them, to the point of knowing which stock you are looking at based on its pattern rather than seeing the symbol.

## Pattern Recognition

Through your consistent chart work, you seek to find patterns from which you may derive a trading strategy. The foundation of pattern recognition is rooted within technical analysis with an emphasis on lateral and angular trend lines. At this point, you have already quantified your style as anticipatory, reactionary, or delayed reactionary and have established your primary methodology of going with the trend or seeking to profit from a trend change. Over time, you will narrow your chart work to individual opportunities. As you grow as a trader, you will not only seek to play basic patterns but the failure of these patterns as well.

## Developing Your Trading Plan (Journal)

Before executing any trade, you must make a note of your read in your trade journal. Write down what you see and why you want to take the trade. Base this on your technical analysis edge and not any qualitative opinion. Within this written plan, quantify your desired trade management before ever executing your trade. By keeping a solid record of your thoughts and your trade-management plan, you will have a detailed account you can look back on and learn.

# Stop Level

Within your trading plan, articulated within your trade journal, you will first identify the level at which your identified setup would no longer be valid. This will become your stop. Using this stop level, you will then calculate your share count, based on your predetermined risk amount. If you are taking a trade in anticipation of a move transpiring, your stop should correlate with the level where the pattern itself is no longer valid. If you are trading reactionary, once a move has already occurred, your stop would be at the point that the pattern reversed (thus making your reactionary entry wrong).

# Share Count

Before placing any trades, use your predetermined risk amount divided by the difference between entry price and your stop price to calculate your share count. After you determine the share count, you can execute the trade. When the trade has been executed, your stop order is entered.

# Profit Levels / Limit Orders

When you have executed your trade, immediately calculate your profit levels based on your original risk per share. You should place limit orders to sell or cover a part of your position to ensure execution once the trade has reached your first predetermined profit level. Some brokers do not allow "bracket orders," where both a stop order and limit order is set at the same time. Contact the service department of your brokerage firm to understand their process if you are unfamiliar with this. Your broker should be more than happy to help accommodate your trading plan. If they are not amenable to your strategy, consider finding a new broker.

# Ongoing Execution

After a trade has been placed and orders entered, you continue to execute your original trading plan. Note your results over a large enough sample set to help you determine areas that might need to be improved.

Let's review an example.

# Example: Mosaic Company (MOS)

As I pursued my daily chart work throughout March 2010, I noticed an angular, ascending trend line in Mosaic Company from October 5, as noted in Figure 16.1. Based on the size of the trend line, I surmised that a break below may lead to a significant drop in share price. I had already noticed significant deterioration in other similar companies such as Monsanto and believed that it may be only a matter of time until this weakness spread to Mosaic. My notes were as follows.

**Journal Entry**

Mosaic has developed a significant angular ascending trend line from October 5. A move below this trend line may result in a further decline in the stock. I desire to take a reactionary short, once the stock breaches this trend line.

**April 9, 2010**

1. Mosaic has dropped below the angular ascending trend line support.

2. Stop above today's high $58.22, actual stop $58.25. (I rounded up my stop level for no other reason than to simplify the math.)

3. Entry at close $56.65 with a $1,000 risk.

4. Stop ($58.25) – entry ($56.65) = $1.60.

5. Total desired risk ($1,000) / risk of trade ($1.60) = Share count (625).

6. Trade taken: Short 625 MOS @ $56.65.

7. Stop entered: Stop 625 MOS @ $58.25.

8. Profit limit entered for 1/3 shares: Buy 208 MOS @ $55.05 (entry price – risk of trade).

## April 16, 2010

1. Covered 208 MOS @ $55.05 (initial realized profit $332.80).

2. Stop lowered to entry $56.65.

3. Profit limit entered: Buy 208 MOS @ $53.45 (entry price − 2x risk of trade).

## April 19, 2010

1. Covered 208 MOS @ $53.45 (partial realized profit $665.60) (total realized profit $998.40).

2. Stop lowered to first profit target $55.05.

**Figure 16.1** *Mosaic breaking below an ascending angular trend.*
Chart courtesy of Worden—www.Worden.com.

This is an example of a trade that worked very well and became quite profitable. Regardless of the outcome, the execution is of utmost importance. If you continuously execute your trading plan, you should see a dramatic difference in your consistency, which should correlate with improved returns. Over time, seek to improve your overall read of the opportunities present and seek to improve your entry strategy as you attempt to maximize your returns while limiting your risk. Incorporate different reads such as trading pattern failure; however, pursue the same execution strategy. As you evolve you will quickly see where your trading needs improvement and where to focus your energy going forward.

# chapter 17

# It's a Head Game

Over the years, I have learned that once you develop and hone your personal trading style, ultimate success has more to do with psychology than any set rule or guideline. Successful trading is the evolution from a battle between man and stocks to a battle between man and himself. Learning to trust certain instincts, avoid others, and stick to a set trading style, all while keeping emotions in check, are just a few of the issues you will face throughout your entire trading career (regardless of how well you understand chart patterns, fundamentals, or macroeconomics).

Therefore, in the subsequent chapters, I discuss ways you can continue to improve your trading excellence. These chapters are concepts I have developed over time and that have helped me tremendously, yet they are not quantifiable within a set trading strategy. My hope is that you find this material of use as you mature as a trader and undoubtedly face new obstacles. Review the chapters once, and then use them as a reference point when specific issues arise (as I know they will).

I firmly believe that should you want to move from good to great, you must be willing to sit and reflect on these outside variables and seek to truly understand how they influence your trading decisions and results. It is a simple matter of getting away from the trading desk to do some personal reflection with the ultimate goal of improving your performance.

It was through this reflection that my style came to fruition. Each step generally started by addressing an issue I was facing, with the result being a new set of rules or guidelines that I followed. Ultimately, I learned that to succeed I had to remove more of me from the equation when an opportunity was identified.

Although I am still honing my strategy on a daily basis, it is the foundation from which I have experienced success and started to achieve my ultimate goal of a consistently rising equity curve with manageable drawdowns.

You must begin by asking yourself some tough questions and seeking real and honest answers. Learning more about yourself, your personality, and the time that you can devote to stock speculation is the first step. After clearly articulating this, you can follow the strategy outlined and thus begin to build your own true pattern of success.

As you embark on this journey, keep in mind that markets should not be viewed as an endless battleground but as an ongoing and continuous world of opportunity from which you can achieve all of your financial goals. You will sometimes experience success, sometimes failure. Instead of becoming discouraged, return to the foundation on which you built your strategy. Move slowly in a methodical way, following each of the steps outlined in this book and honestly assess what part needs special attention. Become a life-long student of your very own trading strategy, seeking mastery and a humble advancement toward profits.

May the tape richly bless you and may your profits exceed your expectations.

# chapter 18

# Dealing with the Emotions

Making money is highly satisfying; by doing so, you gain a sense of accomplishment, and pride can take center stage.

Trading stocks is often portrayed as a high adrenaline, win-lose game in which only the strongest survive. Emotions run wild in a world where money is on the line, and those who can process news the fastest will prevail. Fortunes can be made and lives can be changed, but it takes a no-lose attitude, a fierce drive, and the ability to attack aggressively.

This perception attracts many investors, but it is far from realistic. If you want to pursue this craft longer than a few passionate days, removing more money than you put in, you must be willing to accept the fact that success does not come from mirroring the hyperactive, emotional style I just shared. If you desire to wear a business suit while talking into three phones, that's fine. However, make sure that suit is for taking your spouse out to a fine dinner and you are talking with friends on the phone, because following this appearance-only method won't move you any closer to success in the markets. (It'll just run up the dry-cleaning and phone bill.)

Over the years, I have learned that success in the financial markets actually comes as a result of pursuing just the opposite of what is perceived by the general public. In fact, most successful stock operators spend years attempting to remove emotions (the ups and downs) from their trading. The best traders give absolutely no hint as to how they are doing at the time you interact with them and never allow their performance to alter their lifestyle. In fact, successful trading is often rather boring, and if you find yourself facing consistent emotional swings, odds are you are doing something wrong.

What most traders don't realize when they first set out trading is that they are actually playing the market with two different accounts. The first is tangible, in the form of financial capital and is what most believe to be the only real asset on the line. Another account, however, is even more important than that one. It is your emotional capital, which directly correlates with how you allocate your financial capital and perform on any given day. This emotional capital is what drives you each and every day and allows you to make the appropriate decisions with your financial capital. If this is low or even depleted, you can't possibly make up ground on the financial side (because it takes a full emotional account to start making progress at all).

Whenever I come across a new trader or someone who is ready to adopt a new style, I usually try my best to assess the person's emotional capital to see where he or she stands. I can never just come out and ask, "How's your emotional capital?" If I were to, they'd have no clue what I was talking about. I generally gauge this through subtle clues in the discussion we're having at the time. Most people seek help only when their emotional capital has been depleted and they are ready for a change. I first must help them to rebuild this emotional account before working on any financial gain.

When your emotional capital is low or depleted you may think or say the following:

*I can't do this, I need to just give up and turn my money over to someone else.*

*Every move I make is wrong. Just trade the opposite of me and you'll make money.*

*The moment I sell, it goes up. The moment I buy, it goes down.*

*No one can make money trading stocks over the long haul; it is not possible.*

Your emotional capital becomes depleted because you are trading with no set plan. You have not yet adopted rules that govern your trading, and you are just guessing about what to do or how to trade.

When you are right, you feel as if *you* did something superior and *won*, which boosts your emotions and gives you a feeling of success. When you make a mistake and lose money, you feel like *you* did something wrong and have *lost*. Over time, the financial market will remove money from those guessing.

A trader trading on emotions has absolutely no edge and is therefore fighting a losing battle. You might win sometimes, and sometimes you might lose, but in the long run you will ultimately put more money in than you take out of the stock market.

The flip side is when you resolve to learn the craft and hone in on rules that govern your trading. Your confidence is not found in your ability, but derives from your strategy that has been tested and refined. You must at first trust that your edge works. Over time and through various market cycles, you will soon see this play out and translate into profits. Only then can you start to rebuild your emotional capital that has probably been depleted over the years. When this is done, you can then confidently face the markets without fear or trepidation.

As you pursue this craft, you will inevitably find yourself becoming emotionally drained occasionally. Whether it is through poor execution or Mr. Market dishing out a bit of humility, you are bound to take emotional hits. To deal with this, the first step is to simply recognize this has happened. Articulating to yourself or a trusted friend that you feel your emotional capital running low will immediately bring light to the issue at hand and opportunity to start working on the problem.

It is challenging to begin rebuilding your emotional capital while you are still financially committed to the markets. Fortunately for you, no rule written anywhere says that you must remain in the market at all times. In fact, this flexibility, when embraced, can give you enormous power. Whenever I face a low emotional tank, I immediately move to cash. Many times, I follow up this move by taking at least one day away from the markets. I find it extremely refreshing and helpful to clear my mind, far away from the screens.

After I have regrouped, I then begin to peruse my trading records and journal to identify the root of the problem. Odds are that somewhere along the way my discipline started to falter and I was no longer following my strategy. I ask myself questions such as these:

*Am I imposing my belief on the tape?*

*Am I not pursuing my original trading plan?*

*Am I forcing something that isn't there?*

If I am honest with myself, I typically already know the answers. Throughout my history in trading, there have been times that, for whatever reason, I believed the market should advance or decline. Unfortunately, this belief was not rooted in what the market was doing or what the charts were saying; rather, it was my own opinion. This is natural for most traders. However, acting on these beliefs is where the problems start to occur.

After I have identified the root of the issue—that is, the aspect of my behavior getting in the way of my following a sound strategy— I can then begin to rebuild my emotional tank. I do this very slowly and with a reduced level of risk as I begin to pursue my trading strategy. I start from the very beginning, going through charts with a fresh eye and unbiased view. If a trade emerges that fits my criteria, regardless of whether it correlates with my personal view, I act on what I read, place the trade, and execute my strategy.

Once I get back to the basics, it usually does not take long for me to rebuild my emotional tank. As my emotional capital begins to be restored, I can slowly increase my risk. Before I know it, I am back to account highs and trading better than ever.

Does this cycle ever end? Not to my knowledge. However, the time between emotional account draws does lengthen considerably.

Your goal as a trader should be to execute your strategy and keep your emotions in check at all times. Keeping your emotional account at highs will enable you to increase your financial account. You cannot have one without the other.

# chapter 19

# Following the Trend

I've heard the number one tenet of investing discussed in a variety of ways:

*The trend is your friend.*

*Trade with the wind at your back.*

*Don't fight the tape.* (My personal favorite!)

In just about every trading book you will read, you'll find a core principle admonishing you to always seek to go along with the general market when determining your trade selection. If the general market is trending higher, you should be looking long and willing to buy stocks. If the general market is trending lower, you should be looking to short stocks. The principal is rooted in the fact that markets tend to move in a certain direction for a sustained period of time and that most stocks will follow this trend. In the off chance they might be moving sideways, you will probably hear that you take a step back and wait for the new trend to emerge. A day trader might be concerned with the trend for that particular day only. A swing trader might be concerned with the intermediate trend only or how the market has been moving over the past several weeks. And a passive investor might be concerned only with how the market has been moving over a series of months or even years.

Early in my career, I subscribed to this generalized approach, probably because of how often (and consistently) I saw it discussed. Furthermore, I noticed that when I had a string of losses it typically came from me fighting the general trend. The problem for most investors is how to determine what the general trend is, at the time it is happening. In hindsight, it always seems so simple. You can glance quickly at any chart and see where a stock has been and where it is now to determine the direction of the general trend. When you are trading and seeing the market move on a daily basis, however, this becomes much more difficult. There is always a potential for a great trend change. If the market has been moving higher consistently, you might have a nagging feeling that at any moment the market will plunge to new depths. On the other hand, if the market has been declining, you might believe that at any moment a significant bounce will occur. The internal struggle to actually follow the trend on a consistent basis becomes a big obstacle. Lucky for us, however, there is a simple method that enables us to ensure that more often than not and regardless of time frame we are flowing with the general market. The method I prefer focuses on the 50-day simple moving average.

Moving averages are merely an aggregate of $x$ number of previous days prices filtered into a line graph and plotted on whatever chart you may be reviewing at the time. With a simple moving average, each day's data carries the same weight in the final tally. If we are calculating a 50-day moving average, you add up the closing prices for the preceding 50 days and then divide the sum by 50 to come up with the current plotted amount. When a day is added to the front end, the oldest data is dropped off the back. (Current charts will plot a moving average of your choosing with the click of a mouse.)

I usually review the S&P 500 daily chart to determine where the index is in relation to its 50-day simple moving average. If the index is above this line, I assume the trend is up and I look for buying opportunities. If the index is below this line, I assume the trend is down and I look for shorting opportunities. If the index and its relation to the 50-day moving average suggest a specific direction but this conflicts with my personal view, I do nothing. Since implementing this rule, I have found that I rarely fight the trend; that is, I rarely short stocks as the market is moving higher, or buy stocks as the market is moving lower. Subsequently, this approach has made a significant positive impact on my P&L.

Many traders take this a step further and develop trading strategies around moving averages. I have not found any edge with this. I prefer to just use the moving average as a basic guideline when approaching any trades I may be considering.

Even passive investors taking a longer term approach can immediately improve their results by following a similar guide and reviewing the market in relation to its moving average on a weekly basis to determine whether they should be long the market. Unlike a 50-day moving average, a 50-week moving average plots a line using the previous 50 weeks or almost one year of market movement. Because of this longer-term approach, the line does not change as quickly and can give you a great sense as to what direction the larger trend is heading. As an outside exercise, review the S&P 500 weekly chart along with the 50-week simple moving average over the past 10 years. You will quickly see how adhering to this simple guideline would have taken a passive investor out of the market before both the 2000–2002 decline and the 2008 decline. Once the S&P 500 punctured the 50-week moving average in 2000, it did not recapture this line until May of 2003. Once the S&P 500 punctured the 50-week moving average in 2007, it did not recapture this line until July 2009. Most passive investors would have loved to be out of the market during these two declines. In fact the last puncture of the 50-week moving average was January 2008 and is flirting with another thrust below this level as I am writing this book. I have plotted this on Figure 19.1 for reference.

**Figure 19.1** *S&P 500 in relation to its 50-week moving average.*
Chart courtesy of Worden—www.Worden.com.

Of course, there are times like in 1998 when the market may break this 50-week moving average only to return to this level a few months later before another strong run that goes higher. It is my view that a whipsaw like this is a small price to pay to remain disciplined and protect capital during what may become a significant bear market.

Sometimes my chart work yields trading opportunities in the opposite direction of the general market trend, as noted by the 50-day moving average. Over the years, I have learned to pass on these trades. I typically call these stocks needles in the haystack. Despite what might look like a lucrative opportunity, I have learned that it is much more profitable to trade the haystack.

As you mature as a trader, you might find other indicators to help you determine in which direction the general market is trending. The 50-day simple moving average rule is a basic first step that will ensure you are at least on the proper path. Following this rule will rarely place you on the wrong side of the general market trend.

# chapter 20

# The Blowup

Predicting the unpredictable is the great challenge in trading. It is impossible to be correct all the time, and this is why you implement a system that gives you a slight edge. I have had many profitable months where on review I learned that I had just about the same number of losing trades as I did winning trades. In fact, my winning percentage has sometimes been below my losing percentage and yet I have still managed to eek out profitability.

As a trader, your goal is to execute a system that doesn't seek to eliminate losing trades but rather contain them in a manageable way. It is a system that attempts to capitalize on incremental gains over time while allowing at least a portion of your winning trades to run to their full potential. When executed properly, it will give you a consistently rising equity curve while keeping you sane in the process.

Unfortunately, there will still be times when, regardless of how well you execute, an event occurs in an extraordinary move you did not see coming. I call this the *blowup*. It has happened to every great trader, and as long as you continue down this path, it will happen to you.

One of the tenets of technical analysis is the idea that somewhere someone always knows something that is not yet public. Due to the human emotions of fear and greed, shared by us all, the desire to capitalize on this knowledge becomes far too tempting. It is why you should never be surprised when an unexpected news piece confirms a move that has already taken place. For example, numerous times in my career, I have seen a stock advance wildly despite a negative market. Day after day, the general market may fall while the resiliency of the individual stock stays strong. Even to the novice, it is clear that something is transpiring under the surface that has not yet been made public. Finally, after days or weeks, the news is released that the company is being acquired or that a favorable ruling has come down or maybe even a new product gets launched. I have also seen individual stocks act extremely poor prior to a negative news piece many times, again confirming this price action only after it has already begun. It is not your job to question why this is happening. It is your job to utilize this information to your advantage.

I am often challenged on this subject because people are reluctant to accept the truth that the market will always give you clues in advance, prior to its move. The greatest example I can share of late was the order-routing problem that sparked an intraday 1,000-point drop in the market early in 2010. Most people were taken by great surprise, and countless investors lost fortunes during the slide. Truth be told, the general market had not been acting well far ahead of this debacle and was giving the astute trader more than enough warning signs to step aside. So that I wouldn't get caught in a surprise intraday crash, I was positioned short and capitalized on the fall. Of course, you can never be short enough when a big drop comes, as was the case with me that day. However, it was once again an example of the market talking far before the event transpired.

The blowup is different and comes with no technical warning whatsoever. It is when you have executed your plan extremely well yet something goes wrong and the price action moves significantly in the wrong direction for you. This can happen for a variety of reasons. I have seen companies recall products, face fraud charges, miss earnings, disclose accounting issues, lose contracts, fire executives, or be acquired altogether. All of these resulted in a massive reversal of stock price in an instant.

I believe understanding that this can happen and is part of the game is the first step. As mentioned before, it has happened to all the great traders, and it will happen to you. The question, however, is this: How do you handle the situation when the blowup comes your way?

Nothing is worse than realizing you are on the losing end of a blowup. The loss on the individual trade is far greater than you expected. The pit in your stomach feels like a bowling ball just dropped into it, and the notion of sucking your thumb while hiding under your desk suddenly sounds like it would make for a great day. It makes no difference how you have been trading leading up to the blowup. The event serves as an immediate hit, not only to the financial account but also to the emotional tank.

Through the years, I have learned that when the blowup ensues your natural tendency is to freeze. You begin by hoping the blowup reverses course and that your misfortune will be restored (and so you take no action at all). You immediately are stuck in a hope trade and will more than likely begin watching each and every tick of the stock in question. Your zombie-like state will not only paralyze you from taking action on the particular stock but will hinder you from playing any other areas. Like most things in trading, I believe coming in with a plan already established is the key to not letting a blowup do any lasting damage.

My plan for handling a blowup has evolved over time. My primary goal has remained the same: remove the position as quickly as possible so that I can psychologically and financially accept the loss. After the position has been removed, I then move forward looking to repair the financial damage in other areas. Whenever I face a blowup, I immediately take off one-half of the position. It makes no difference to me why the blowup has transpired. I do not argue with the price action in front of me. Nor do I add money to this position seeking to improve my price. Several years ago, when blowups transpired, I sought to remove the entire position immediately. Over time, I noticed that whereas most stocks never returned to where they were before the blowup, some did improve from their initial price immediately following the blowup. Based on this observation, I decided to hold at least one-half throughout the day with the goal of removing the balance at day's end.

It makes absolutely no difference to me where the stock is trading after the blowup occurs. I want out of the name by day's end. I never adjust my trading plan when something transpires that wasn't originally suggested in the chart. To pursue this path would be the beginning of my demise.

Once the position has been removed from the account, I no longer review the stock. In many instances, the stock in question quickly repairs all the damage in short order. If you become infatuated with the price action of your blowup stock after you have moved out, you run the risk of remaining emotionally attached. If you see the stock bounce back significantly, you might hesitate the next time this happens, hoping for a similar outcome. Unfortunately, your hesitation might lead to even greater financial deterioration that cannot be quickly and easily repaired.

I have also witnessed several occasions where the stock in question never returns to the pre-blowup price, and in many instances the company even goes out of business. My goal as a trader is to be always in motion, seeking new opportunities for my capital. I do not want to endlessly torture myself by watching a stock that is dead money.

It always amazes me how quickly I can repair the financial damage once the blowup stock has been removed. Throughout my career, I have been on the losing end of a blowup on many occasions, and you will as well. However, I have been able to overcome the obstacle each time. My rule in handling the blowup remains firm and simple, and I encourage you to adopt a similar method.

Of course, you can incorporate some nuance into your trading to seek to limit the number of blowup instances. Throughout the years, I have collected and implemented several ancillary rules I live by in my day-to-day trading. These rules have helped me avoid blowups significantly and may be something to consider for your trading, as well.

# Earnings

Four times a year, publicly traded companies are required by law to report earnings. At these times, the market can resemble a casino. Depending on the mood of the market at the time, stocks may be rewarded handsomely or punished severely. It is not enough just to assume that if a company reports better-than-expected earnings its stock will subsequently rise. Nor is it a safe assumption that a company reporting a worse-than-expected quarterly result will be punished. You must get into the habit of checking when your stocks report so as to not be caught off guard. A company's earnings report is usually a catalyst for a large move, and your success should never depend on guessing this outcome.

My rule is simple. I never hold more than one-third of a full position in a stock through a company's earnings announcement. This remains true regardless of where I am in the trade at the time. In fact, I prefer to not hold any shares at all and will pass on a trading opportunity if I see their earnings release is too close to the date for which I'm pondering the trade.

Adhering to this rule allows me to avoid potentially damaging results. Earnings season is a breeding ground for blowups, and I would rather avoid these if I have the choice.

As you trade, you might be tempted to gamble on an earnings report of a specific company. I strongly encourage you to avoid this at all costs. Regardless of whether your opinion is correct, it can easily breed a bad habit, which, if allowed to take hold, can prove extremely damaging.

I am always amused when I see someone making a big bet on an earnings announcement. I am even more amused when I see someone boasting of success, as if some sort of skill set allowed the person to capitalize on the opportunity. I shake my head, knowing it is only a matter of time before this person becomes just another statistic on the failure of traders in the marketplace.

# Special Events

Similar to earnings announcements, there will be certain times a special event will become a market-moving catalyst. This may be an FOMC (Federal Open Market Committee) meeting, an employment report, or a government change. It will be very clear this event will have the power to move the market and alter stock prices significantly. It is my rule to reduce my exposure dramatically prior to this taking place.

I view these events much like gambling, with very little edge for the astute trader. Rather than bet on the outcome, I prefer to see how the action transpires. Once the news is known and digested, I can again assess the landscape and seek out new opportunities.

# Biotechnology

Over the years, I have become increasingly wary of one particular stock group: biotechnology. Biotechnology seeks to blend medicine with technological advancements and is often a playground for intense speculation. The group is governed by the FDA (Food and Drug Administration), which has the power to make or break a company overnight.

I have seen companies advance several thousand percent on the heels of a favorable FDA ruling, just as I have seen a company lose 70% of its market cap on a negative ruling.

At times, the potential for gains is enticing, but I generally choose to avoid the sector altogether. For every solid winner, it has been my experience that there are four or five terrible losers. Most of the time, the charts of these companies give you little hint about their next movement, with the most bullish turning extremely bearish and vice versa.

I have yet to regret not playing this sector, and on many instances have been thankful that I stayed away. I would consider removing this group from your playlist and avoid the potential for great disaster through the next biotech blowup.

As time progresses, there may be new areas or events to consider avoiding. As a trader, you must embrace the fact that one trade should never be able to make or break your account. Let others travel this dangerous path while you simply grind out consistent gains in a boring manner.

# index

# H

Halliburton, 142-143
handling blowups, 195-199
head and shoulders pattern, 29, 59
head games, 181-182
higher lows, 68
house money, 158

# I

IBM, 144-145
    stop strategy example, 135
    trend lines, 63, 68
inflection points, 62-63
*The Intelligent Investor* (Graham
    and Dodd), 12

# J-K-L

journals, 97-107, 174

lateral trends, 61-66, 72
level one traders, 5
level three traders, 6
level two traders, 5
limit orders, 176

# M-N

market opportunities, recognizing
    and embracing, 19-23
MeatBaron, 101-102
Mosaic Company (MOS), 176-179
moving averages, 189-193
NASDAQ 100
    2002-2008, 74
    charting, 65

# O

O'Neil, Bill, 15
opportunities, recognizing and
    embracing, 19-23
other traders, analyzing actions
    of, 25-32

# P

pattern failure, 146
pattern recognition
    backing and filling, 28
    bearish wedge pattern, 31
    bullish cliff pattern, 31
    cup and handle pattern, 58
    fractal nature of, 85-87
    head and shoulders pattern,
        29, 59
    overview, 58, 174
    trend lines
        *angular trends, 66-69*
        *Chesapeake Energy
            example, 74*
        *explained, 57-60*
        *Exxon Mobile example, 73*
        *Fifth Third Bancorp
            example, 71-72*
        *lateral trends, 61-66*
        *NASDAQ 100 from
            2002-2008, 74*
        *Potash example, 72*
        *trading strategies and
            capital deployment
            methodologies, 73*